ADVANCED TONAL DICTATION

ADVANCED TONAL DICTATION

Thomas L. Durham
Brigham Young University

WAVELAND PRESS, INC.
Long Grove, Illinois

For information about this book, contact:
   Waveland Press, Inc.
   4180 IL Route 83, Suite 101
   Long Grove, IL 60047-9580
   (847) 634-0081
   info@waveland.com
   www.waveland.com

Copyright © 2005 by Waveland Press, Inc.

10-digit ISBN 1-57766-355-1
13-digit ISBN 978-1-57766-355-3

All rights reserved. No part of this book may be reproduced, stored in a retrieval system, or transmitted in any form or by any means without permission in writing from the publisher.

Printed in the United States of America

8   7   6   5   4   3   2

TABLE OF CONTENTS

Preface — vi

Focus

Section 1 (CD 1) — PITCH — Review of intervals — 2
RHYTHM — Beat values and divisions
METER — Simple duple
HARMONY — Secondary dominants of the dominant

Section 2 (CD 7) — PITCH — Augmented unison — 14
RHYTHM — Beat subdivision, dotted values
METER — Simple duple
HARMONY — Secondary dominants of the supertonic and subdominant

Section 3 (CD 13) — PITCH — Augmented seconds — 26
RHYTHM — Beat values, divisions and subdivisions
METER — Compound duple
HARMONY — Secondary dominants at the mediant and submediant

Section 4 (CD 19) — PITCH — Augmented fourths — 38
RHYTHM — Beat values and divisions
METER — Simple triple
HARMONY — Leading tone secondary dominants of the dominant

Section 5 (CD 25) — PITCH — Diminished fifth — 50
RHYTHM — Beat divisions, subdivisions, dotted values, syncopation
METER — Simple triple
HARMONY — Leading tone secondary dominants of supertonic and subdominant

Section 6 (CD 31) — PITCH — Review intervals — 62
RHYTHM — Beat values, divisions and subdivisions
METER — Compound triple
HARMONY — Leading tone secondary dominants of the mediant and submediant

Section 7 (CD 37) — PITCH — Diminished fourths — 74
RHYTHM — Beat, values and divisions
METER — Simple quadruple
HARMONY — Neapolitan sixth

Section 8 (CD 43) — PITCH — Diminished seventh — 86
RHYTHM — Dotted values, borrowed values and divisions
METER — Simple quadruple
HARMONY — Italian sixth

Section 9 (CD 49) — PITCH — Augmented sixth — 98
RHYTHM — Beat values, divisions, borrowed values
METER — Compound quadruple
HARMONY — French sixth

Section 10 (CD 55) — PITCH — Compound intervals — 110
RHYTHM — Beat values and divisions
METER — Complex meters
HARMONY — German sixth

INDEX TO EXERCISES AND CD TRACKS — 122

PREFACE

Advanced Tonal Dictation, follows the format, style, and pedagogical approach of its predecessor, ***Beginning Tonal Dictation***. Written for the second year (usually third semester) of aural studies, it contains a regulated group of pitch, rhythm, melodic and harmonic dictation exercises designed for use in and out of the classroom. **This manual differs from other ear training books because students can check their work immediately–they cover the answer to the left with a piece of scratch paper, and remove it to check their work.**

Although theory and ear training programs vary from school to school, teachers unanimously affirm the importance of dictation (aural) skills in music education. The ability to *hear with the eye and see with the ear* separates the most able musicians from the average. Dictation exercises prevail as the best gauge of aural acuity. These exercises boil down to three basic skills: writing out a rhythmic succession, a melodic succession, and a harmonic progression. This manual focuses on those skills only, leaving other peripheral exercises to alternate authors and texts.

Advanced Tonal Dictation has ten chapters or "sections." Each section has a FOCUS which concentrates on a particular intervallic, rhythmic, metric, and harmonic concept (see Table of Contents). Students hear the instructor play an example, write out what was played, then compare their answers against the instructor's key. This process eliminates the instructor's time-consuming task of calling out the detailed answers, and provides for immediate feedback to the student.

In each section, pitch, rhythm, and melodic exercises appear before the harmonic materials. **In all exercises, students should take a piece of scratch paper, and cover up the "Instructor's Key" until they are ready to check their answers.** The following instructions will benefit those using this text:

PITCH

Students write out the second, third, and fourth notes of three tetrachords. The first note of the exercises is given to the student. Instructors may wish to ask the student to identify the three intervals that result from the tetrachord.

RHYTHM

Students hear the instructor play an eight bar melody and are given beginning, halfway, and ending note values in a staff with a neutral (rectangular) clef. Then they write out only the rhythm of the melody. This rhythm features a particular pattern mentioned in the FOCUS. Similar patterns will occur in the melody below the rhythm exercises. These exercises feature a mixture of meters, note values, rests and ties as mentioned in the FOCUS.

MELODY

Having completed the pitch and rhythmic portions of the exercise, students now write out an eight measure melody which combines the pitch and rhythmic concepts of previous exercises. Some notes at the beginning, middle and end are given to the students as a reference. As with the rhythmic exercises, the melodic exercises feature the same mixture of meters, note values, rests and ties.

HARMONY

The harmonic dictation exercises follow. Students listen to a group of from four to seven chords, writing them out on a grand staff provided to the right of the answers. The first chord is given in its four-part spacing. The instructor may have the class write out all four parts, only the outer voices, or merely the Roman numeral analysis. If the class finds the exercise too difficult, the instructor may give them a chord or two along the way, or parts of chords.

A variety of keys and ranges is used, and the examples become increasingly longer and more difficult. Each section contains a subheading "A" for major keys and "B" for minor. All sections focus on a particular chord, group of chords, or inversion. The students are expected to retain past concepts because any chord previously encountered might appear later in the exercises.

TO THE INSTRUCTOR

Because dictation can sometimes become monotonous, you may wish to vary your approach to the use of these materials. The following suggestions will diversify your normal routine:

1. **Error Detection**–Prior to class, add some accidentals to the pitch exercise, change the rhythm exercise in a few places, and modify a few pitches and rhythms in the melody. Then ask the students to watch the instructor's page and locate errors in the exercises as you play the "wrong" version through.

2. **Error dictation from memory**–Prior to class, prepare the pitch, rhythm and melody exercises as in #1 above. This time, have the students close their books as you play the example with the wrong notes or rhythms you added. The students should then open their books, look at the exercise you played and then *from memory* attempt to identify the errors.

3. **Interval identification** –Play the tetrachord examples but instead of having the students write down the notes, have them identify the interval chain instead.

4. **Harmonic error detection**–As in #1 above, alter a few of the notes in a harmonic dictation exercise and ask the students to locate the error.

5. **Harmonic error detection from memory**–Prepare a harmonic dictation exercise as in #4 above. Again, (as in #2 above) have the students close their books as you play the example, wrong notes and all. Then have the students open their books and mark the errors *from memory*.

6. **Separate voices** –Instead of having the students write out the harmonic dictation in four parts, ask them to write out only the tenor, or any other single part. Or have them complete the outer voices, the inner voices, or any combination of voices.

7. **Harmonic scramble**–Have the students examine a harmonic exercise on the instructor's page. As you play the example, scramble the order by playing the chords *out of sequence* in a predetermined order. The students should write "1" below the first chord played, "2" below the second and so on. Blanks already exist for this exercise because these spaces are normally used for the analysis of the chord above when taking harmonic dictation.

8. **Non-harmonic tones**–As the students watch the instructor's page in a harmonic dictation exercise, add two or three non-harmonic tones to the exercise, and ask the students to identify them, write them in, or both. Outer voices tend to be easier than inner voices, so be sure to include examples of each.

TO THE STUDENT

These materials can be used outside of class by using the accompanying CD. This disk contains all the odd numbered exercises found in the book. Recorded exercises bear a "**CD**" designation of some sort. The index at the back of the book will help you match particular exercises with numbered CD tracks. Each track contains a group of three exercises all found on the same page–either a pitch/rhythm/melody group, or three harmonic dictation examples. Use your pause, memory, fast forward, and rewind functions freely on your CD player to customize your practice session.

Another valuable method of practice involves two students assisting each other. One can play the role of the instructor at the piano while the other practices dictation examples from the book. If a student has already filled in the rhythm and melody answers on a particular page, it might be useful to reverse the rhythm and melody examples when practicing outside of class. In other words, have your partner play the melody exercise while you write down its rhythm, then listen to the rhythm exercise and write down its melody on a blank sheet of music manuscript paper. Both rhythm and melody were composed with the principles of the FOCUS in mind, and are interchangeable for practice. (You may wish to adapt this idea while using the CD's by yourself.) Any quiet room with a piano gives ample privacy for such a session.

Any student can improve his or her aural skills, but ear training takes patience. Understand that with time and practice, improvement will come. The time it takes will be justified by the satisfaction you feel with improved aural acuity. Although these skills are not music in themselves, they will significantly inform the music you write, analyze, conduct, and perform.

ACKNOWLEDGMENTS

This book benefitted from the generous assistance of colleagues, students instructors, teaching assistants, and hundreds of students at Brigham Young University. In addition, the University Press of America granted permission for the author to use his own harmonic progressions from an earlier publication under their copyright.

The author also expresses his gratitude to Zachary Herries, whose skills as a recording engineer, and meticulous attention to detail, made the production of the accompanying CD to this volume possible.

ADVANCED TONAL DICTATION

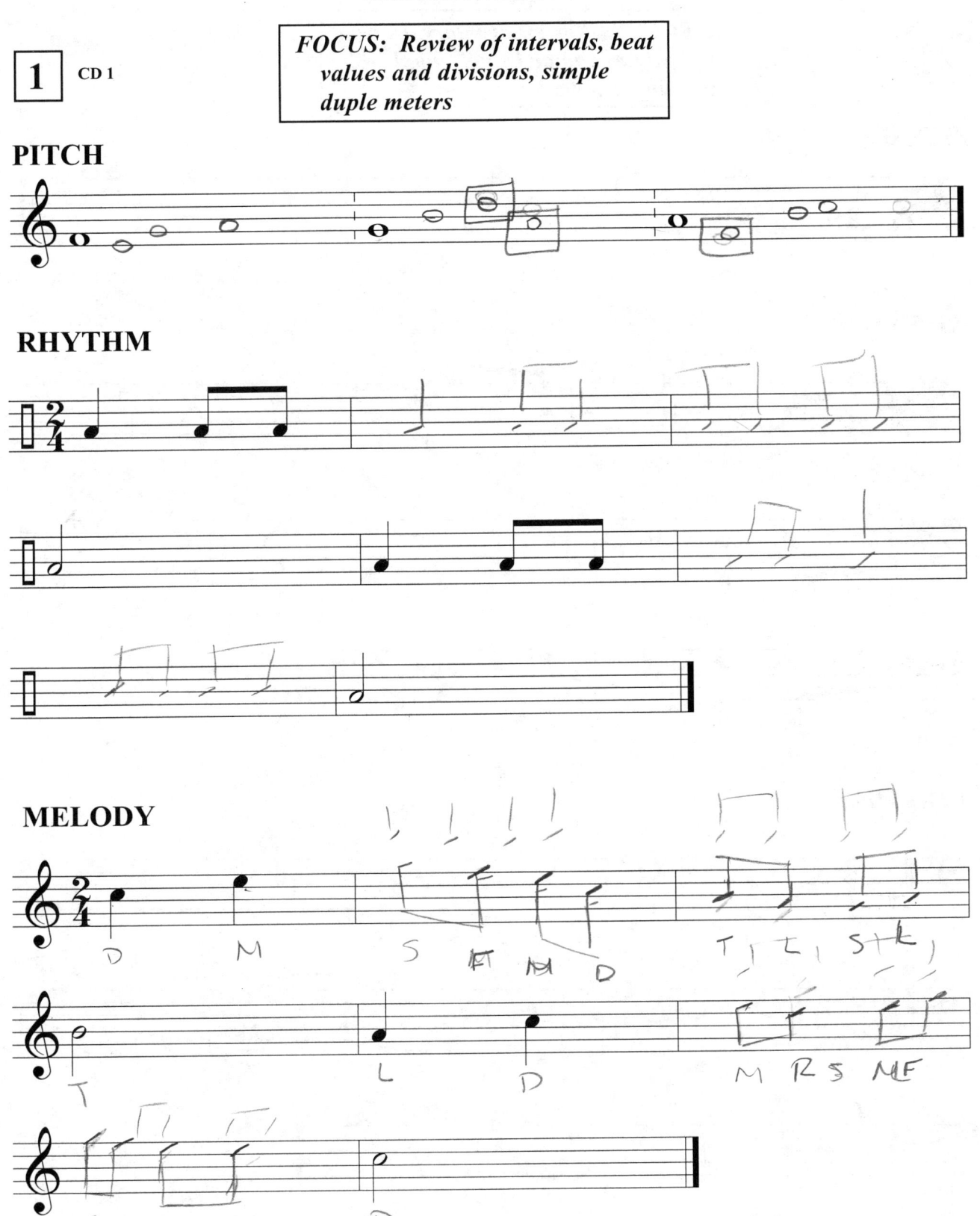

SECTION 1
Instructor Key

FOCUS: Review of intervals, beat values and divisions, simple duple meters

2

PITCH

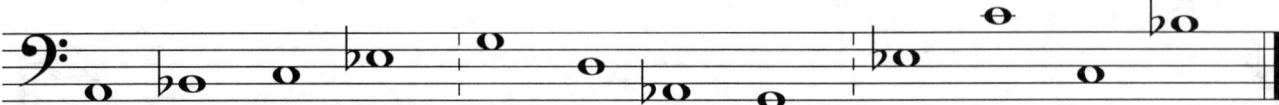

RHYTHM

MELODY

SECTION 1
Student Answer

2

FOCUS: Review of intervals, beat values and divisions, simple duple meters

PITCH

RHYTHM

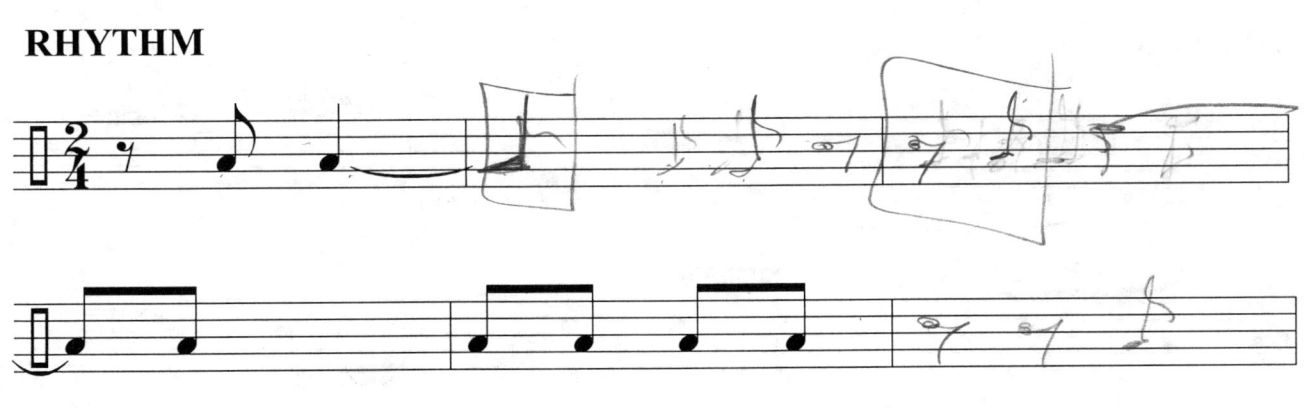

MELODY

SECTION 1
Instructor Key

 CD 2

FOCUS: Review of intervals, beat values and divisions, simple duple meters

PITCH

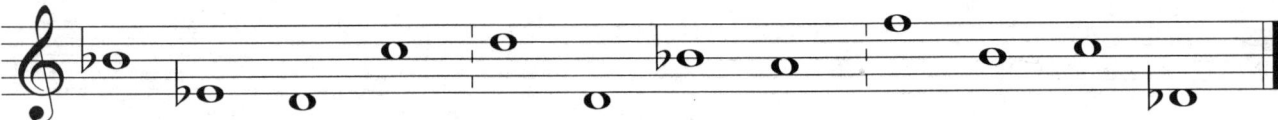

RHYTHM

MELODY

SECTION 1
Student Answer

FOCUS: Review of intervals, beat values and divisions, simple duple meters

7

SECTION 1
Instructor Key

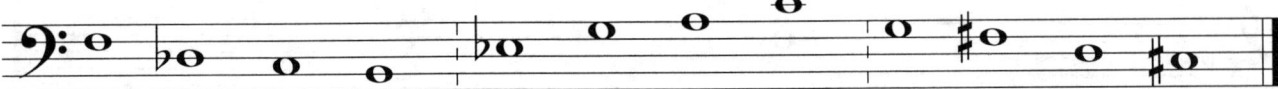

4

FOCUS: *Review of intervals, beat values and divisions, simple duple meters*

PITCH

RHYTHM

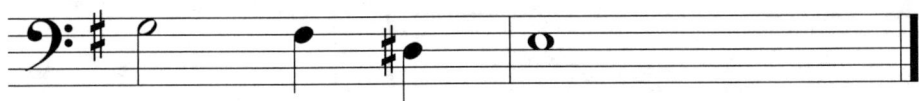

MELODY

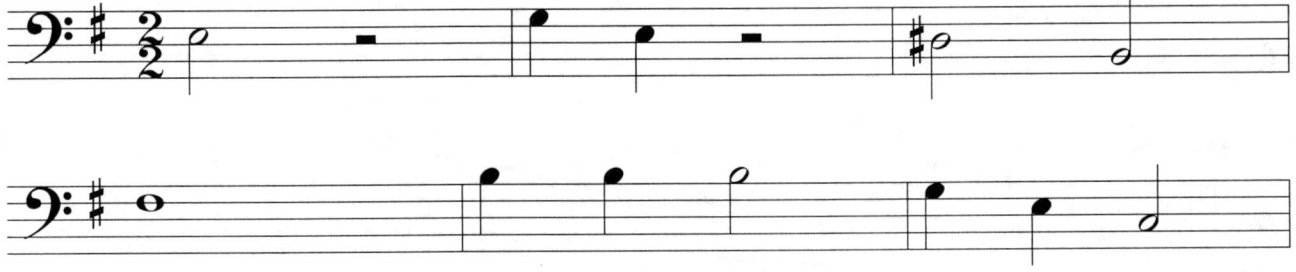

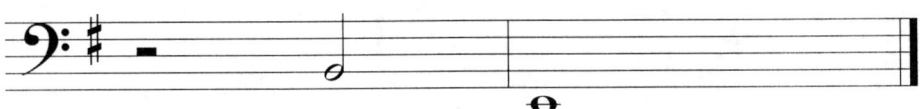

SECTION 1
Student Answer

4

FOCUS: Review of intervals, beat values and divisions, simple duple meters

PITCH

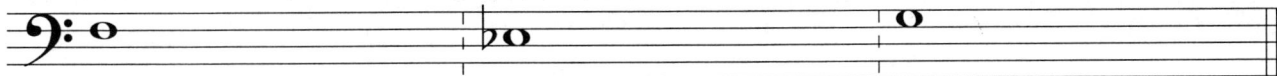

RHYTHM

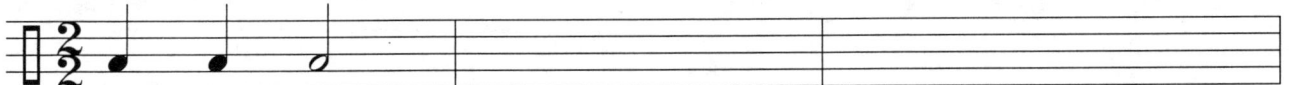

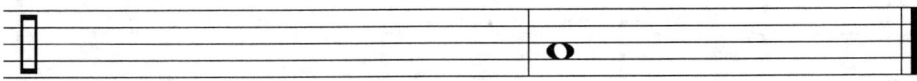

MELODY

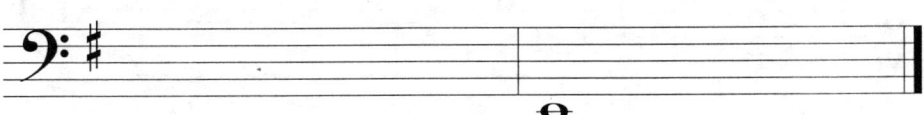

SECTION 1A
Harmony

FOCUS: *Secondary dominants of the dominant*

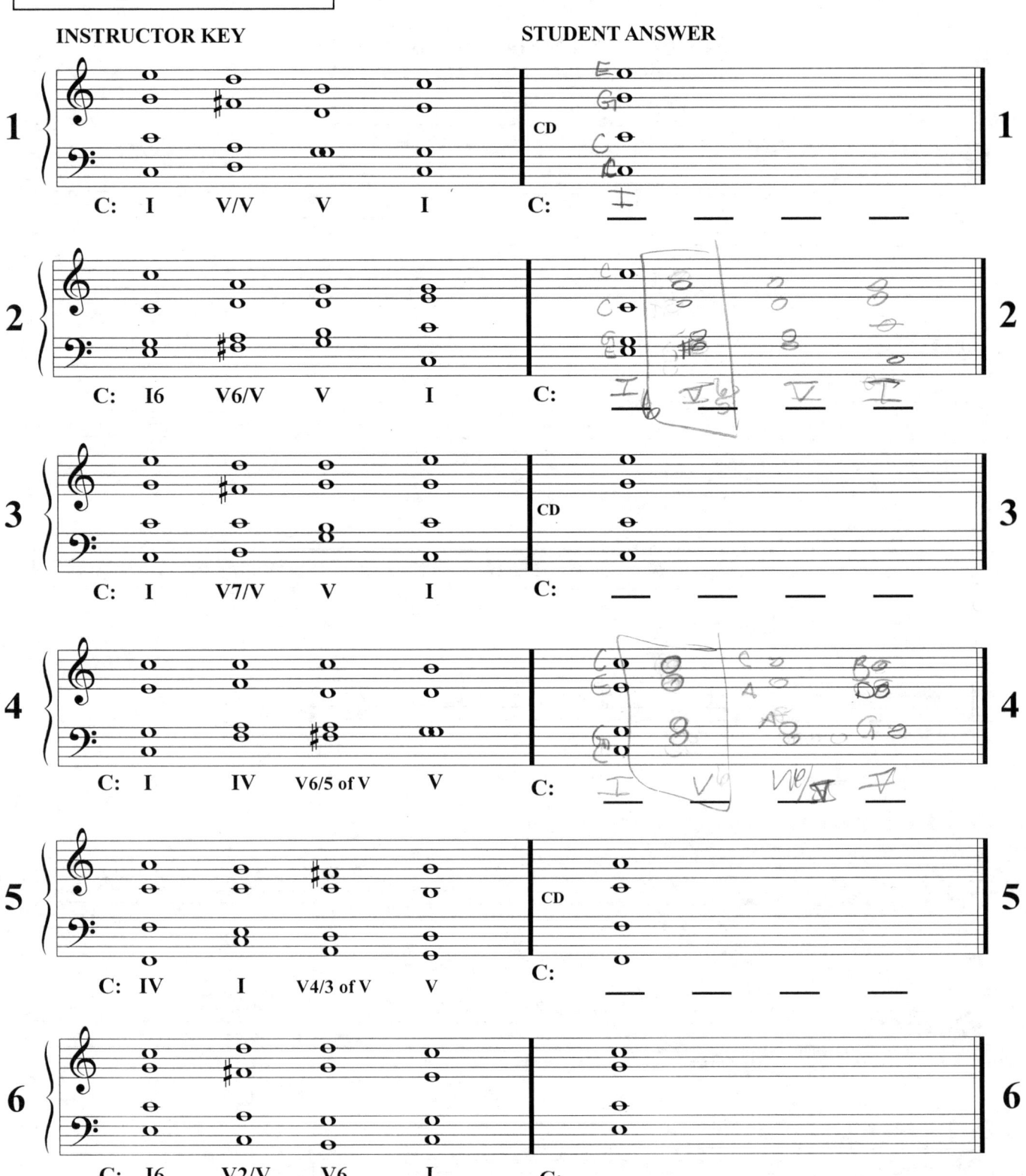

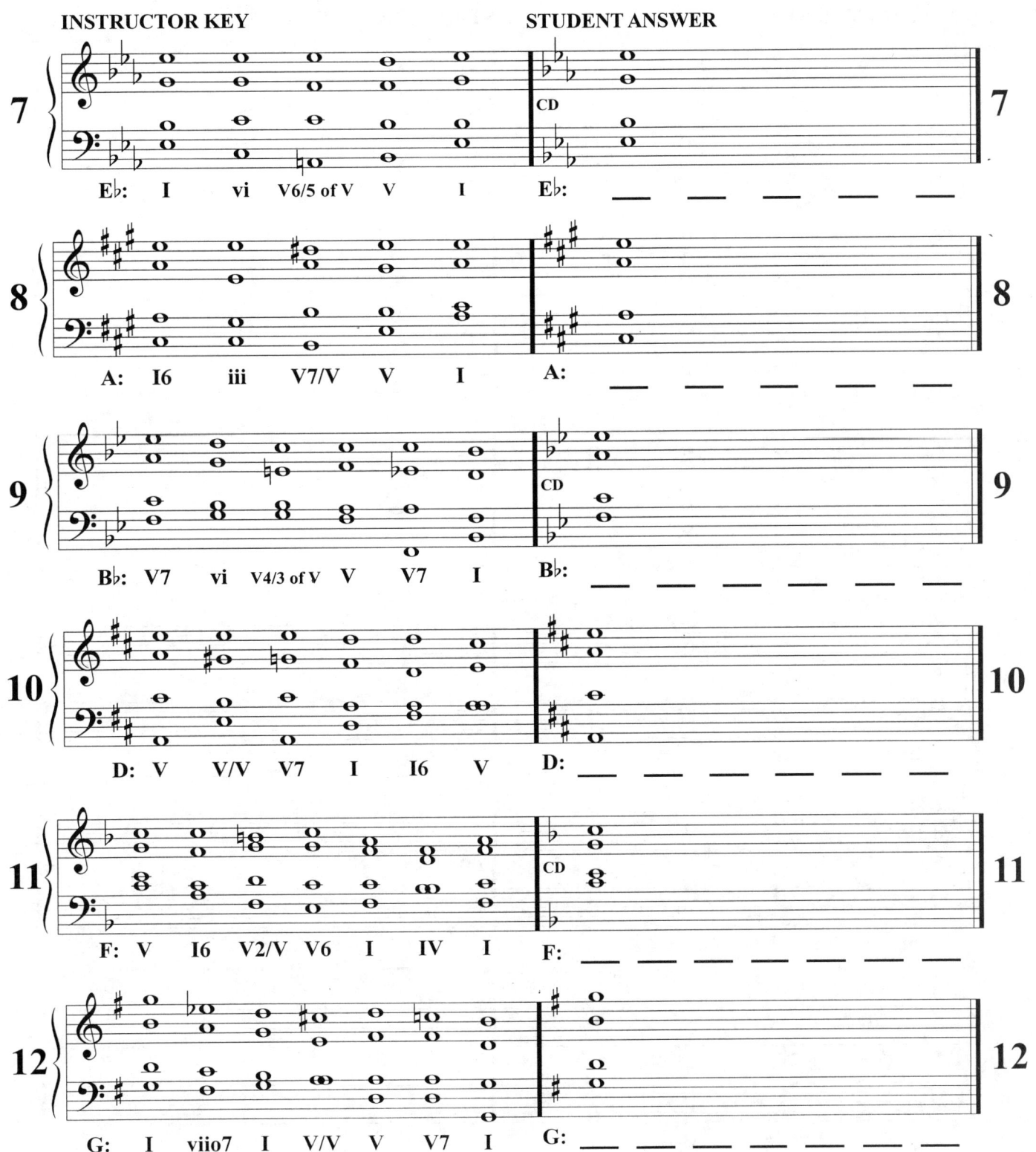

CD 5

SECTION 1B
Harmony

FOCUS: *Secondary dominants of the dominant*

INSTRUCTOR KEY — STUDENT ANSWER

1. a: i   V/V   V7   i   ‖ a: ___ ___ ___ ___
2. a: i   V7/V   V   V   ‖ a: ___ ___ ___ ___
3. a: i   V7/V   V6/5 of V   V   ‖ a: ___ ___ ___ ___
4. a: i   iv   V6/5 of V   V   ‖ a: ___ ___ ___ ___
5. a: i   VI   V4/3 of V   V   ‖ a: ___ ___ ___ ___
6. a: i   V2/V   V6   i   ‖ a: ___ ___ ___ ___

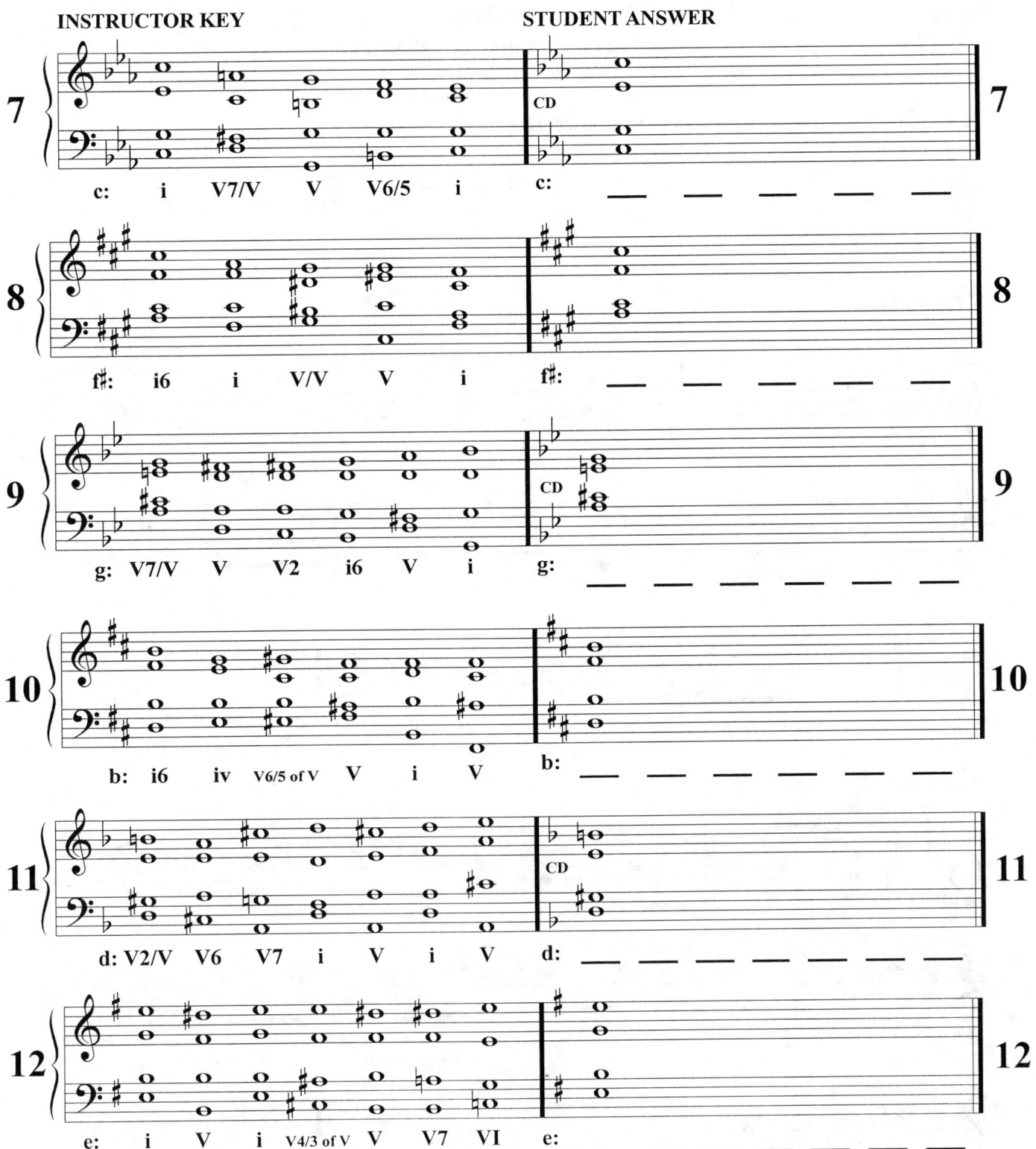

SECTION 2
Instructor Key

FOCUS: Augmented unison, beat subdivisions, dotted values, simple duple meters

1 CD 7

PITCH Note: enharmonic equivalents are correct

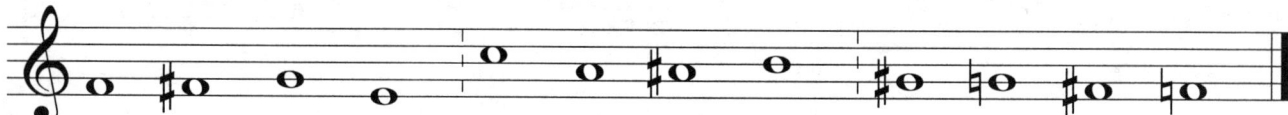

RHYTHM

MELODY

SECTION 2
Student Answer

1 CD 7

FOCUS: Augmented unison, beat subdivisions, dotted values, simple duple meters

PITCH   Note: enharmonic equivalents are correct

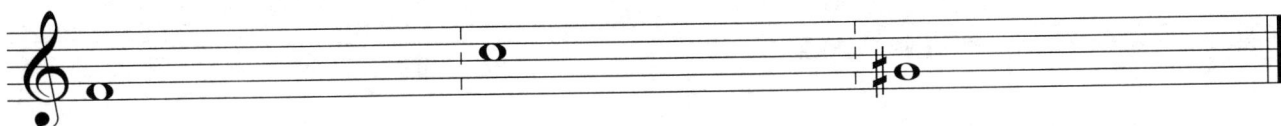

RHYTHM

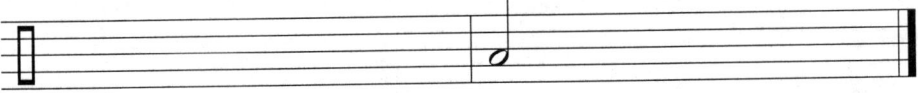

MELODY

15

SECTION 2
Instructor Key

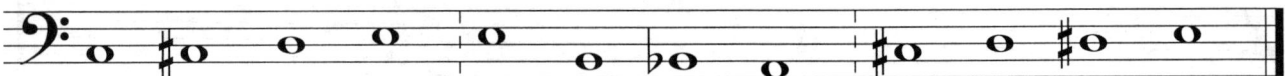

PITCH Note: enharmonic equivalents are correct

RHYTHM

MELODY

SECTION 2
Student Answer

> *FOCUS: Augmented unison, beat subdivisions, dotted values, simple duple meters*

2

PITCH Note: enharmonic equivalents are correct

RHYTHM

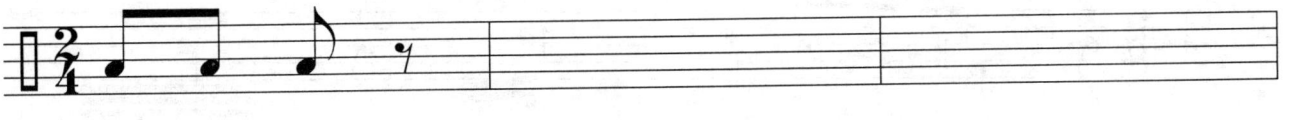

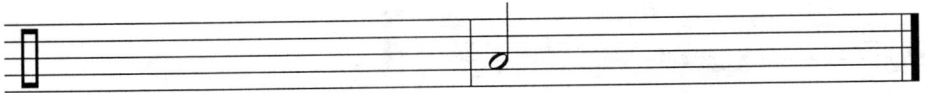

MELODY

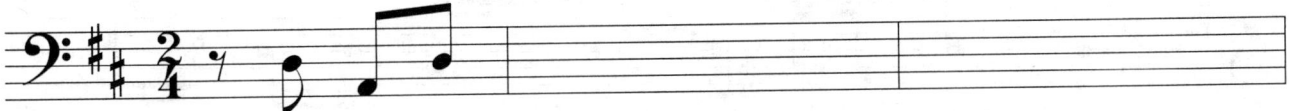

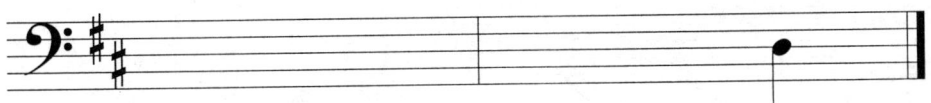

SECTION 2
Instructor Key

3 CD 8

FOCUS: Augmented unison, beat subdivisions, dotted values, simple duple meters

PITCH Note: enharmonic equivalents are correct

RHYTHM

MELODY

SECTION 2
Student Answer

3 CD 8

FOCUS: Augmented unison, beat subdivisions, dotted values, simple duple meters

PITCH Note: enharmonic equivalents are correct

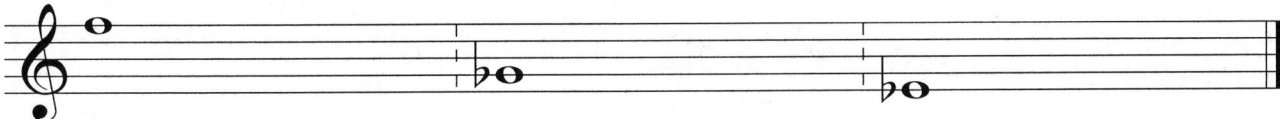

RHYTHM

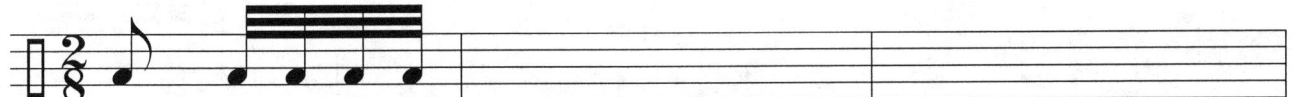

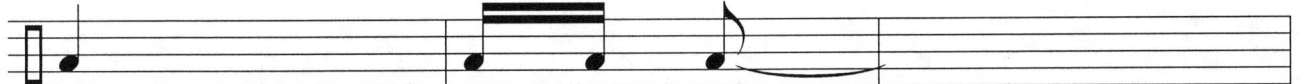

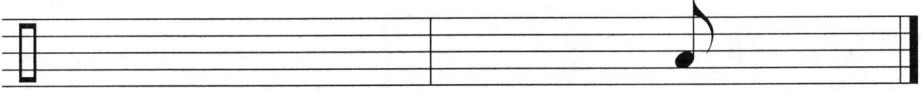

MELODY

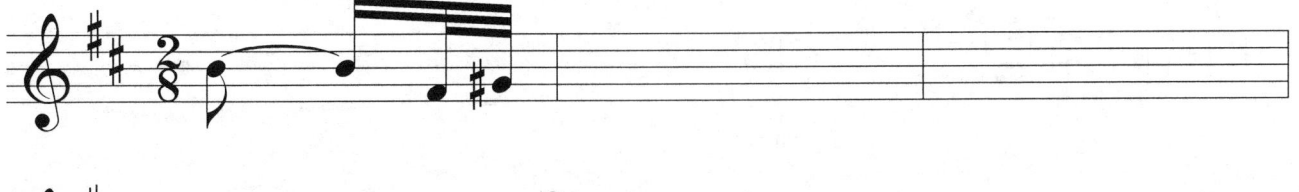

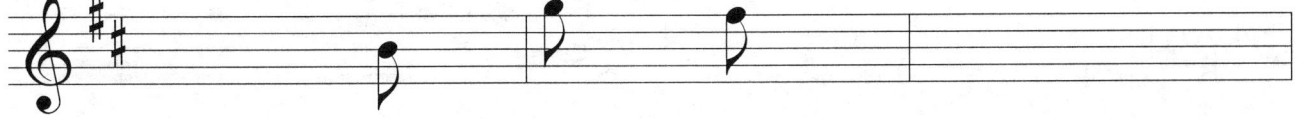

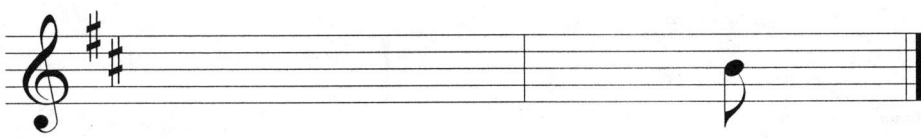

SECTION 2
Instructor Key

4

FOCUS: Augmented unison, beat subdivisions, dotted values, simple duple meters

PITCH   Note: enharmonic equivalents are correct

RHYTHM

MELODY

SECTION 2
Student Answer

> *FOCUS: Augmented unison, beat subdivisions, dotted values, simple duple meters*

4

PITCH   Note: enharmonic equivalents are correct

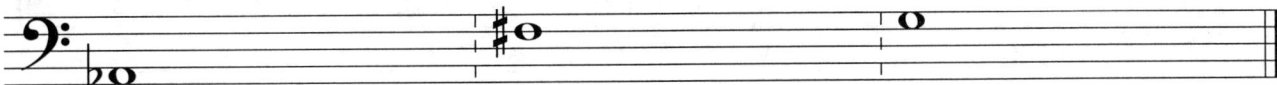

RHYTHM

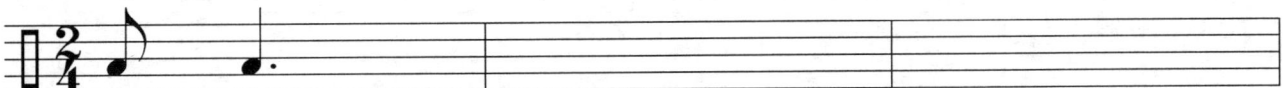

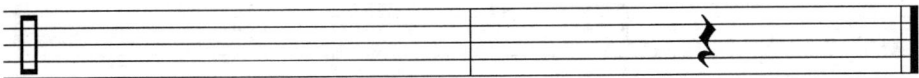

MELODY

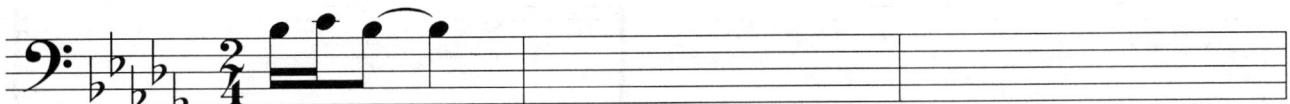

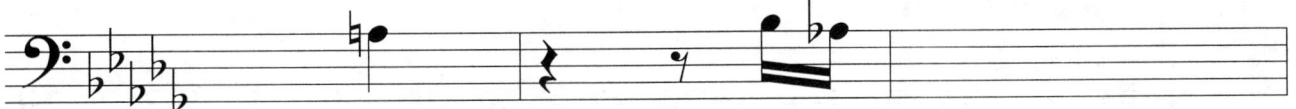

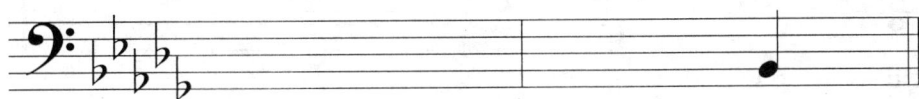

CD 9

SECTION 2A
Harmony

FOCUS: *Secondary dominants of the supertonic and subdominant*

INSTRUCTOR KEY   STUDENT ANSWER

1. C: I   V7/ii   ii   V   C: ___ ___ ___ ___

2. C: V7/IV   IV   I   I   C: ___ ___ ___ ___

3. C: I   V6/5 of IV   IV   I   C: ___ ___ ___ ___

4. C: V7/ii   V6/5 of ii   ii   V   C: ___ ___ ___ ___

5. C: I   V4/3 of IV   IV   I   C: ___ ___ ___ ___

6. C: I   V4/3 of ii   ii   V   C: ___ ___ ___ ___

22

SECTION 2A
Harmony

FOCUS: *Secondary dominants of the supertonic and subdominant*

INSTRUCTOR KEY — **STUDENT ANSWER**

7. E♭: V7/ii V2/ii ii6 V I
   E♭: ___ ___ ___ ___ ___

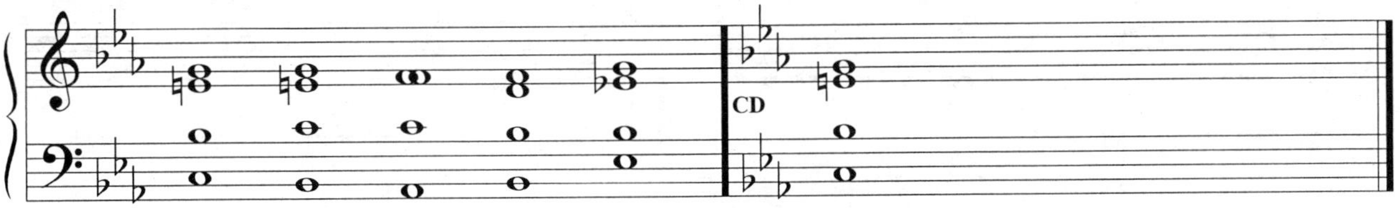

8. A: IV I V7/IV IV V7
   A: IV I V7/IV IV V7

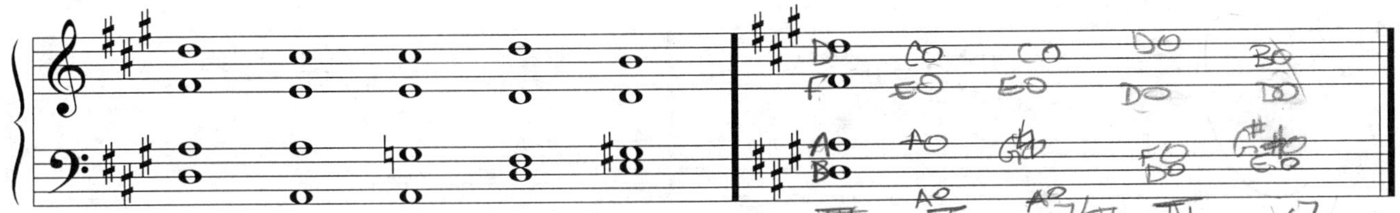

9. B♭: V V7/ii ii ii6/5 V I
   B♭: ___ ___ ___ ___ ___ ___

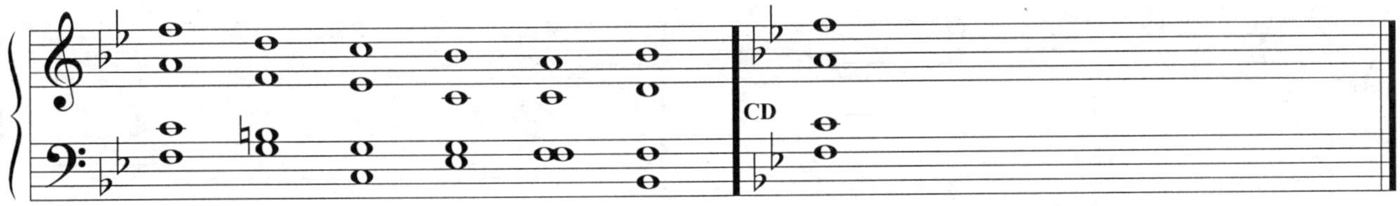

10. D: I6/4 V7 I V6/5 of ii ii V
    D: I6/4 V7 I V6/5 (ii) ii V

11. F: I V4/3 I6 IV V2/ii ii6 V
    F: ___ ___ ___ ___ ___ ___ ___

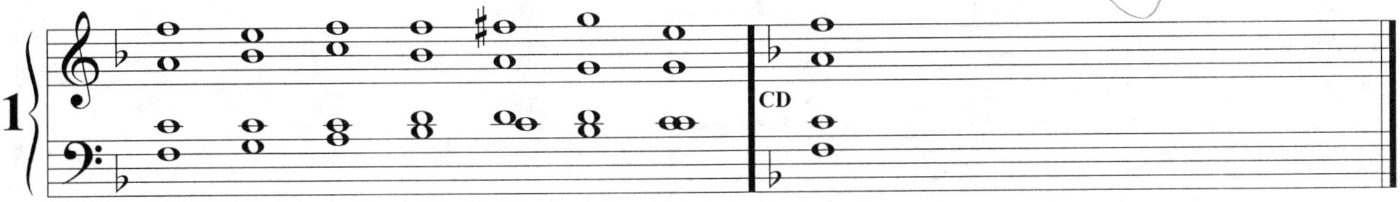

12. G: I IV V4/3 of IV IV I vi V
    G: I IV V4/3 IV I vi V

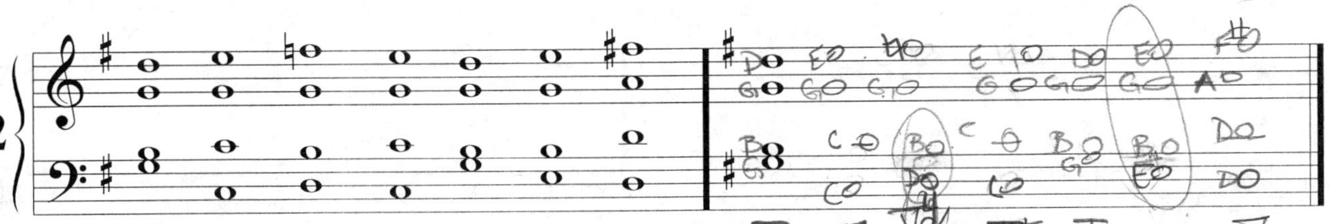

23

SECTION 2B
Harmony

FOCUS: *Secondary dominants of the supertonic and subdominant*

INSTRUCTOR KEY — **STUDENT ANSWER**

1. a: i — V7/iv — iv — i | a: ___ ___ ___ ___

2. a: i — V7/ii — ii — V | a: ___ ___ ___ ___

3. a: V7/iv — iv — i — V | a: ___ ___ ___ ___

4. a: V6/5 of ii — ii — V7 — i | a: ___ ___ ___ ___

5. a: i — V — V4/3 of iv — iv | a: ___ ___ ___ ___

6. a: i — V7/ii — ii — V | a: ___ ___ ___ ___

SECTION 2B
Harmony

FOCUS: *Secondary dominants of the supertonic and subdominant*

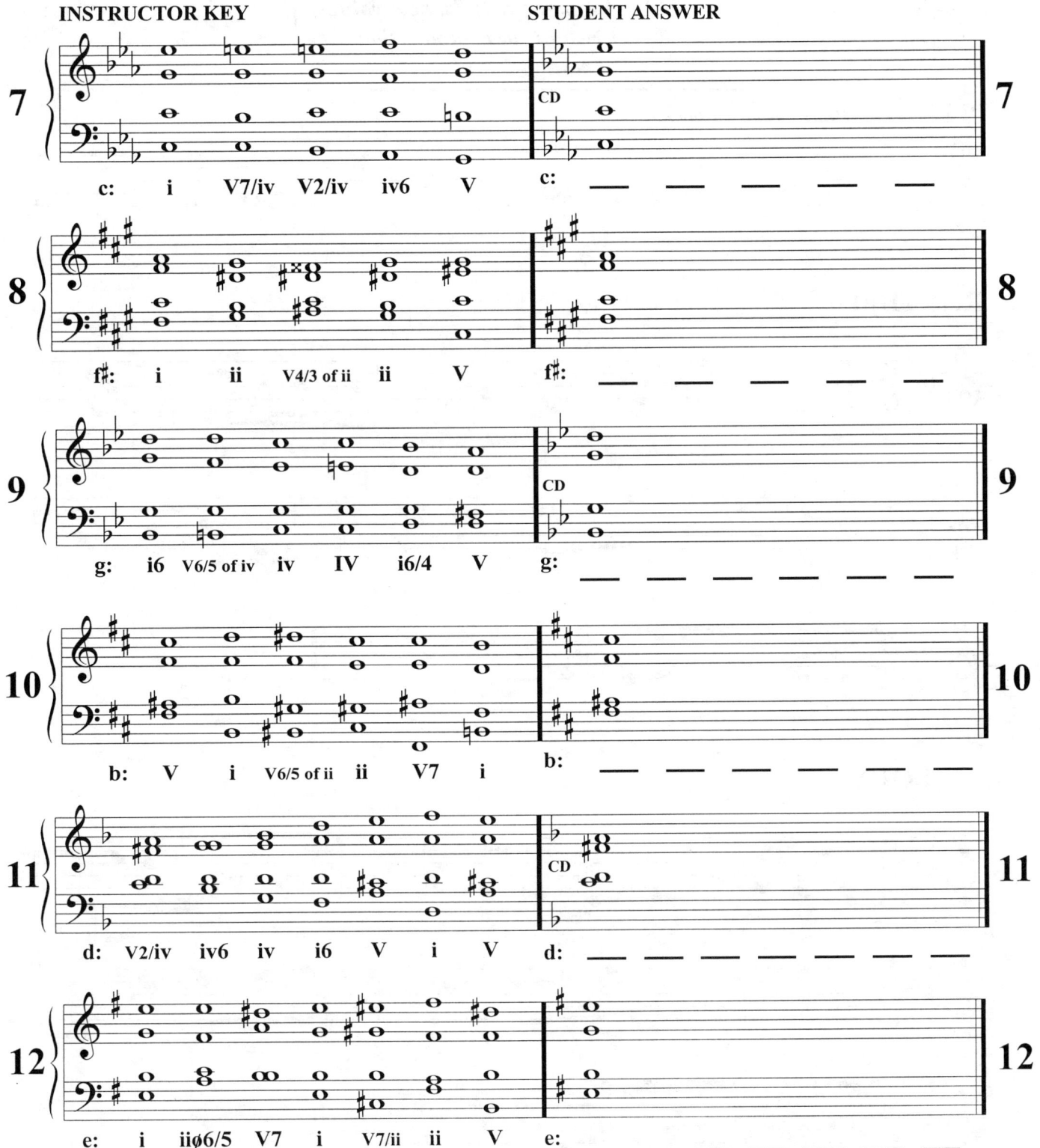

SECTION 3
Instructor Key

1 CD 13

FOCUS: *Augmented 2nds, beat values, divisions and subdivisions; compound duple meters*

PITCH *Hint: Listen for the A2*

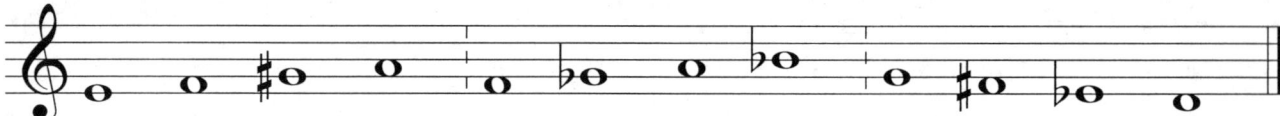

RHYTHM

MELODY

SECTION 3
Student Answer

1 CD 13

FOCUS: Augmented 2nds, beat values, divisions and subdivisions; compound duple meters

PITCH   *Hint: Listen for the A2*

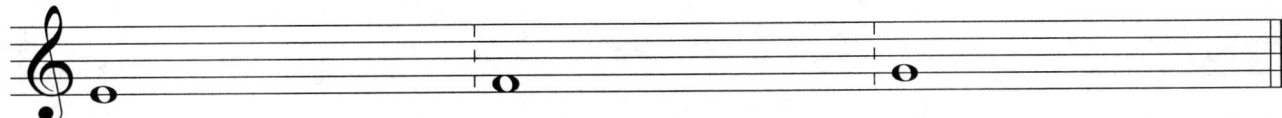

RHYTHM

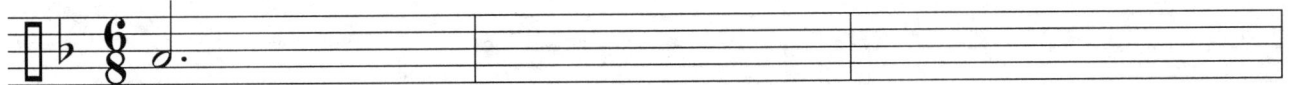

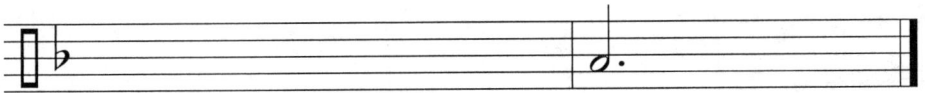

MELODY

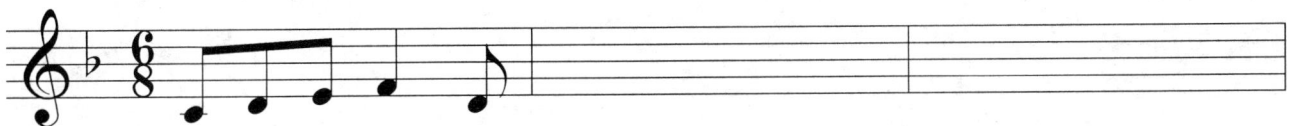

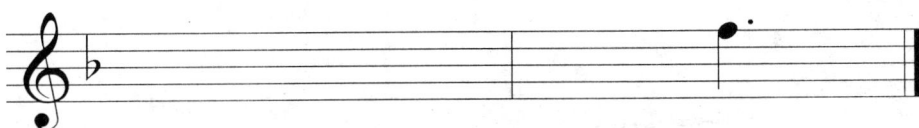

SECTION 3
Instructor Key

FOCUS: Augmented 2nds, beat values, divisions and subdivisions; compound duple meters

2

PITCH   *Hint: Listen for the A2.*

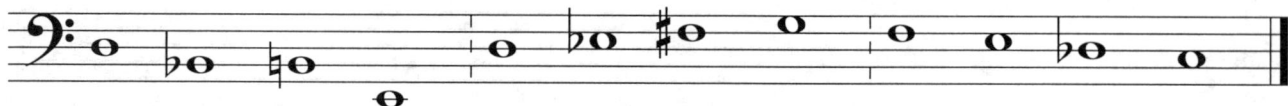

RHYTHM

MELODY

SECTION 3
Student Answer

> *FOCUS: Augmented 2nds, beat values, divisions and subdivisions; compound duple meters*

2

PITCH   *Hint: Listen for the A2.*

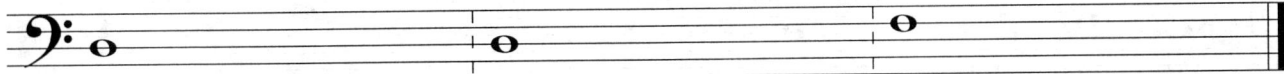

RHYTHM

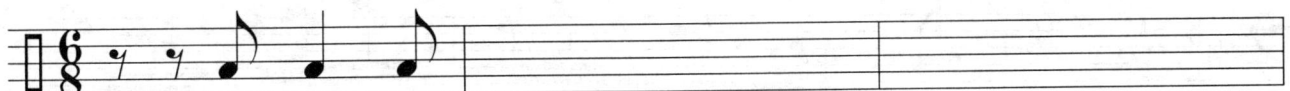

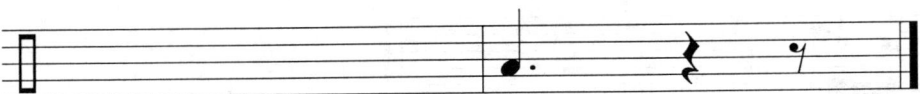

MELODY

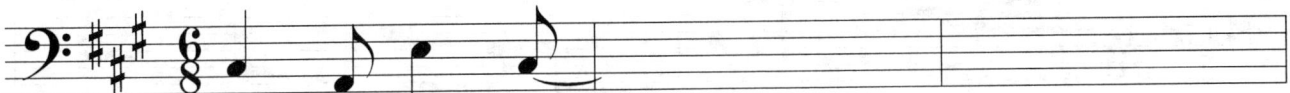

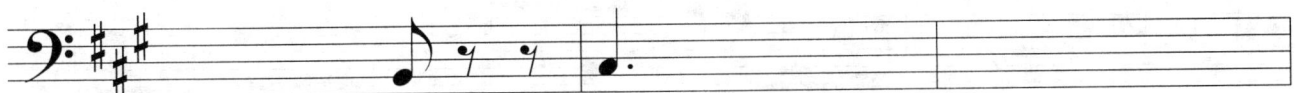

SECTION 3
Instructor Key

> *FOCUS:* Augmented 2nds, beat values, divisions and subdivisions; compound duple meters

3 CD 14

PITCH *Hint: Listen for the A2.*

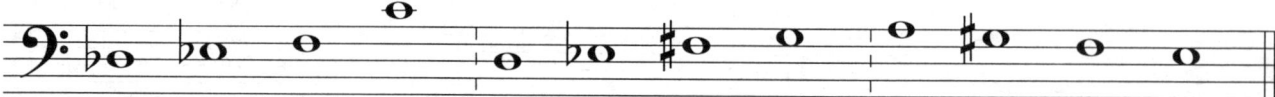

RHYTHM

MELODY

SECTION 3
Student Answer

> FOCUS: Augmented 2nds, beat values, divisions and subdivisions; compound duple meters

3 CD 14

PITCH   *Hint: Listen for the A2.*

RHYTHM

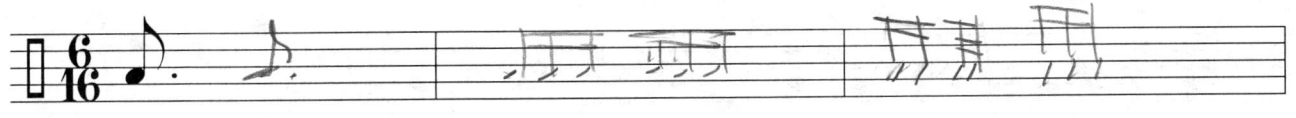

MELODY

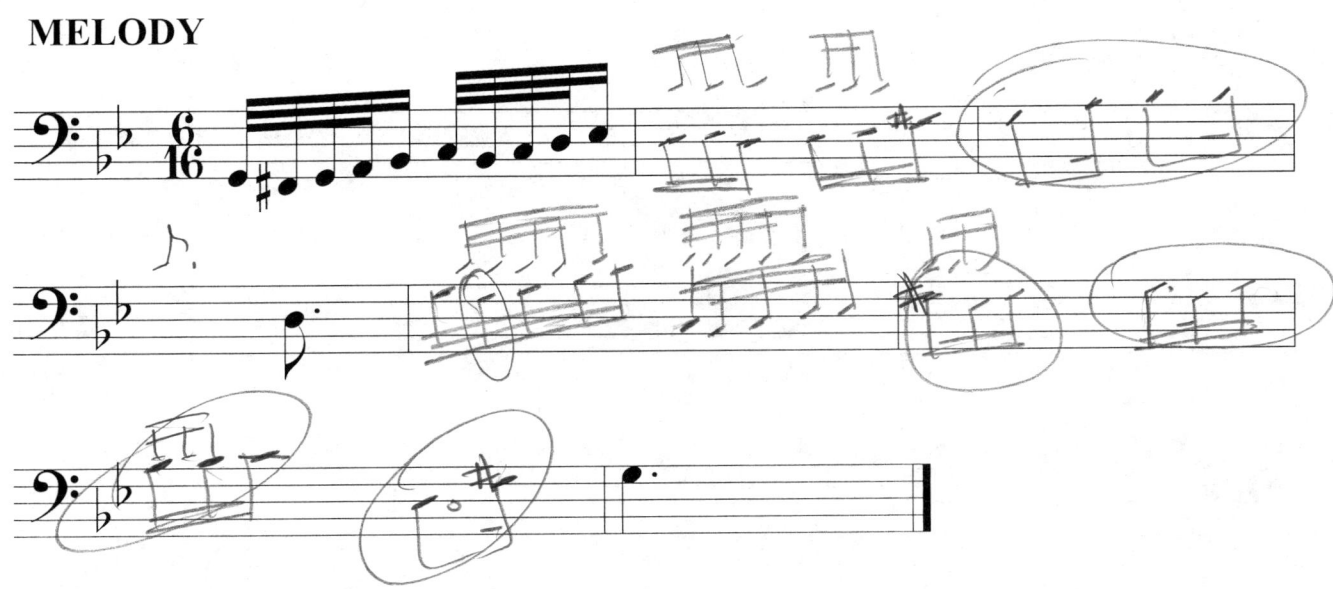

31

SECTION 3
Instructor Key

> FOCUS: Augmented 2nds, beat values, divisions and subdivisions; compound duple meters

4

PITCH   *Hint: Listen for the A2.*

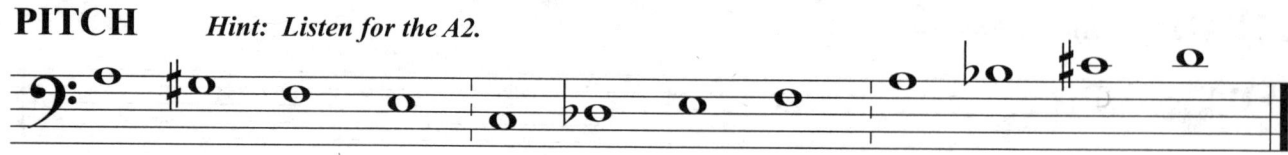

RHYTHM

MELODY

SECTION 3
Student Answer

FOCUS: Augmented 2nds, beat values, divisions and subdivisions; compound duple meters

4

SECTION 3A
Harmony

FOCUS: *Secondary dominants of mediant and submediant*

INSTRUCTOR KEY

1. C: I — V7/vi — vi — V
2. C: V7/iii — iii — iv — I
3. C: I — vi — V7/iii — iii
4. C: I6 — V7/vi — vi — V
5. C: I6 — I — V4/3 of vi — vi
6. C: I6 — IV — V4/3 of iii — iii

STUDENT ANSWER

1. C: __ __ __ __
2. C: __ __ __ __
3. C: __ __ __ __
4. C: __ __ __ __
5. C: __ __ __ __
6. C: __ __ __ __

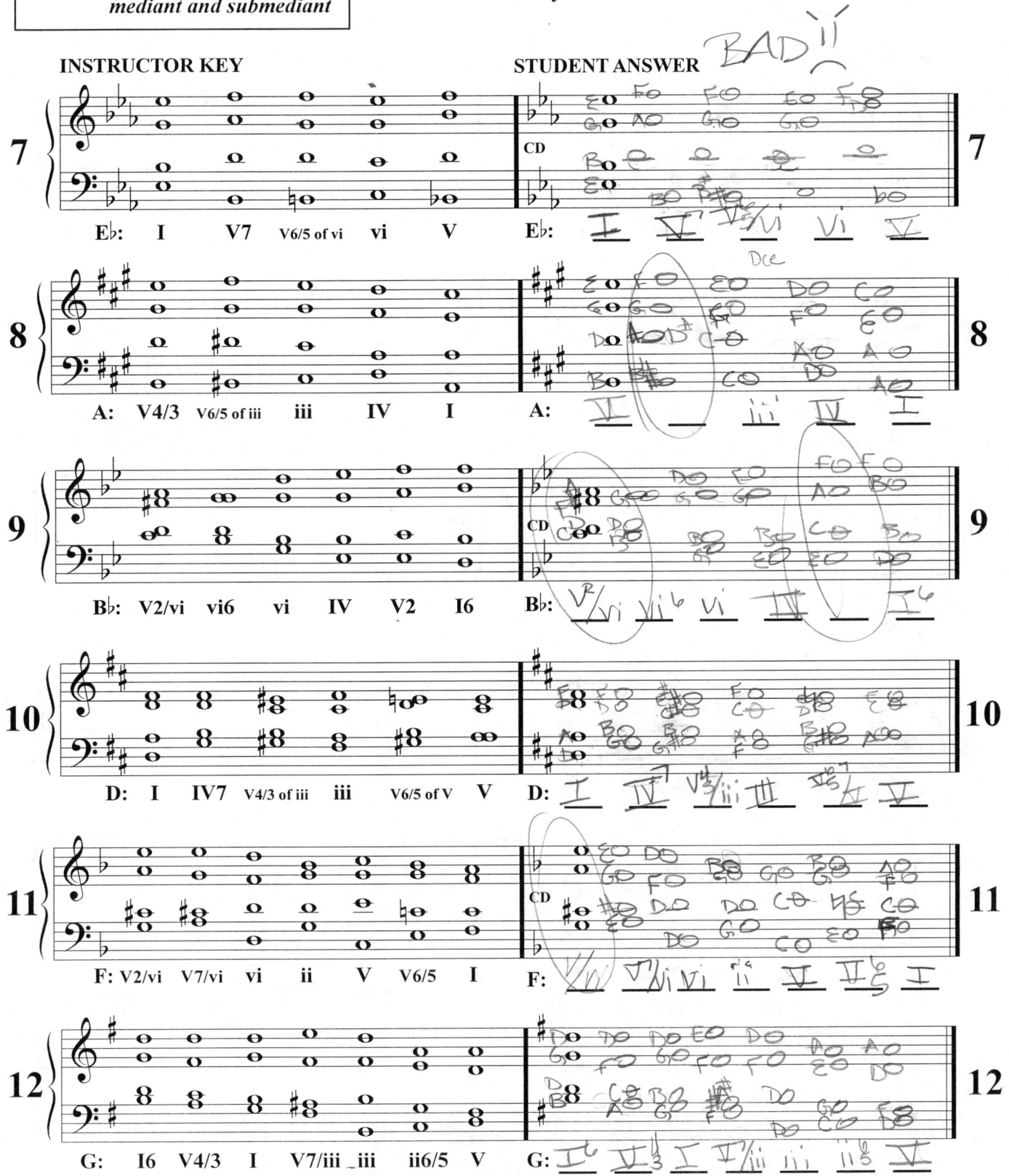

SECTION 3B
Harmony

FOCUS: *Secondary dominants of the mediant and submediant*

CD 17

INSTRUCTOR KEY — **STUDENT ANSWER**

1. a: i — V7/III — V6/5 of III — III | a: ___ ___ ___ ___

2. a: i — V7/VI — VI — iv | a: ___ ___ ___ ___

3. a: i — III — V7/III — III | a: ___ ___ ___ ___

4. a: i — VI — V6/5 of VI — VI | a: ___ ___ ___ ___

5. a: i — V6/5 of III — III — iv | a: ___ ___ ___ ___

6. a: V2/III — III6 — iv6 — i | a: ___ ___ ___ ___

CD 18

SECTION 3B
Harmony

FOCUS: *Secondary dominants of the mediant and submediant*

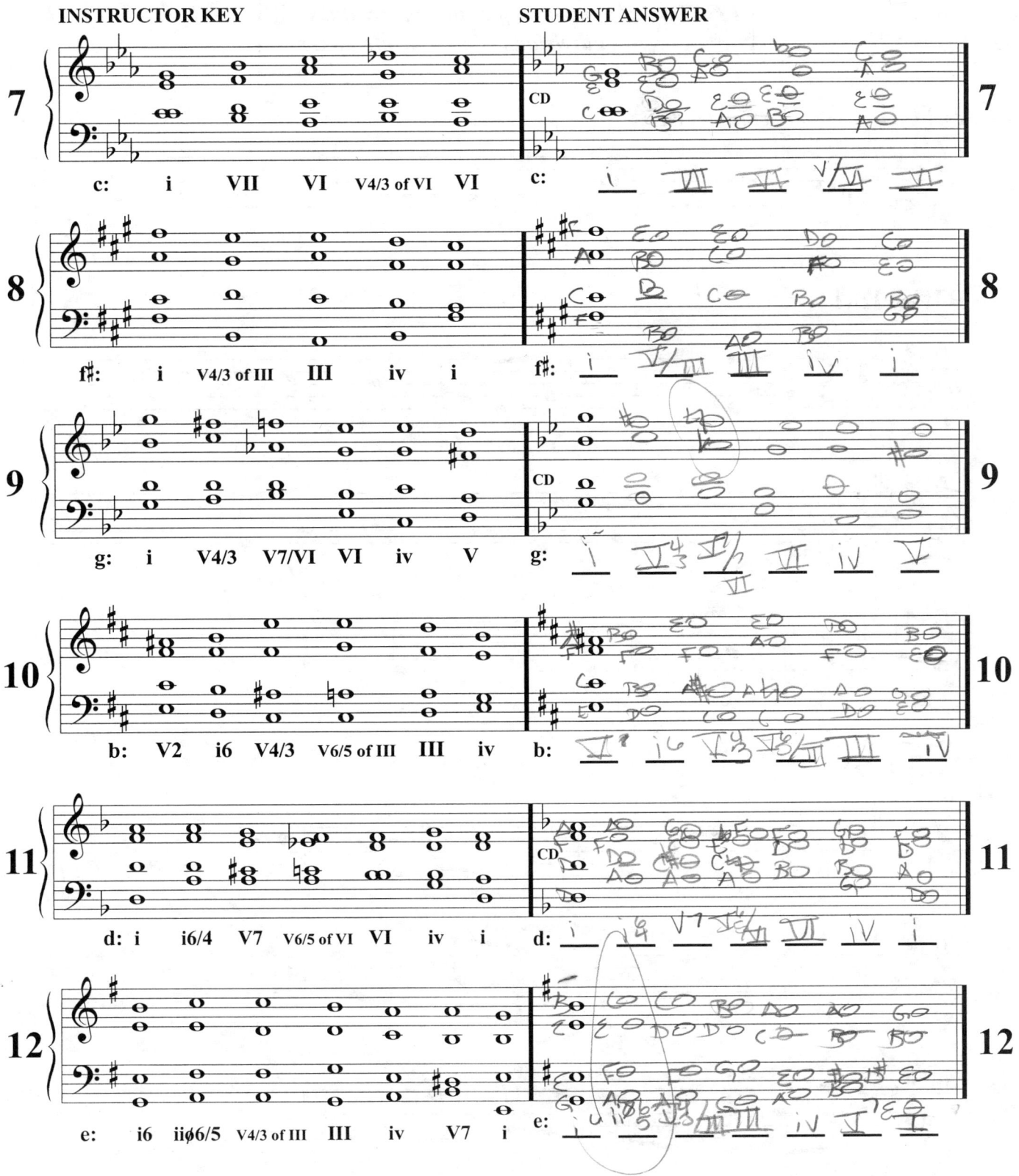

SECTION 4
Instructor Key

FOCUS: Augmented fourths, beat values and divisions, simple triple meters

PITCH   *Hint: Listen for the A4.*

RHYTHM

MELODY

SECTION 4
Student Answer

1 CD 19

FOCUS: Augmented fourths, beat values and divisions, simple triple meters

PITCH *Hint: Listen for the A4.*

RHYTHM

MELODY

SECTION 4
Instructor Key

2

FOCUS: *Augmented fourths, beat values and divisions, simple triple meters*

PITCH   *Hint: Listen for the A4.*

RHYTHM

MELODY

SECTION 4
Student Answer

SECTION 4
Instructor Key

3 CD 20

FOCUS: Augmented fourths, beat values and divisions, simple triple meters

PITCH *Hint: Listen for the A4.*

RHYTHM

MELODY

SECTION 4
Student Answer

FOCUS: Augmented fourths, beat values and divisions, simple triple meters

3 CD 20

PITCH   *Hint: Listen for the A4.*

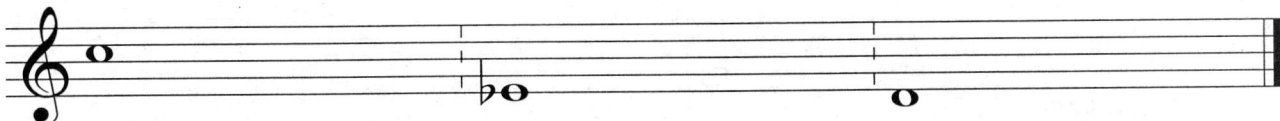

RHYTHM

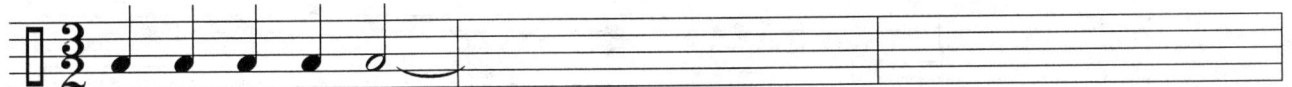

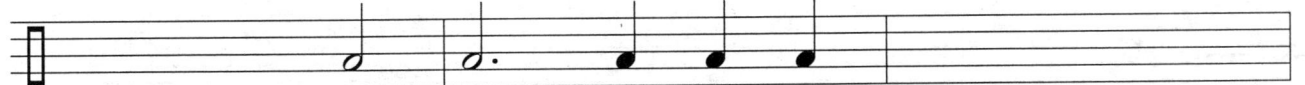

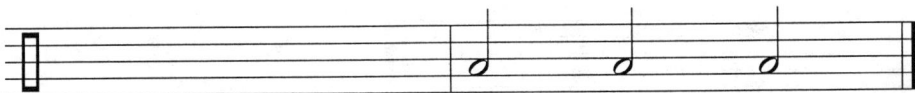

MELODY

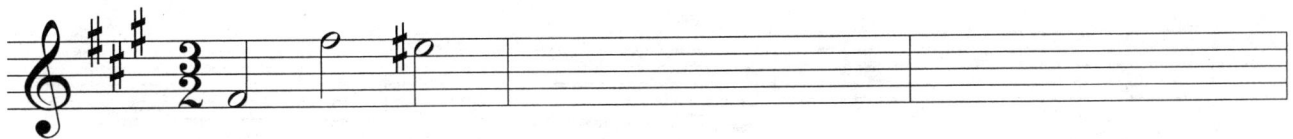

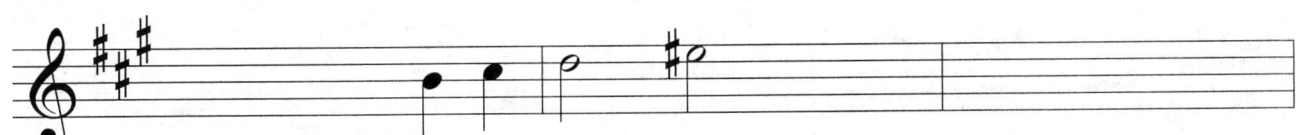

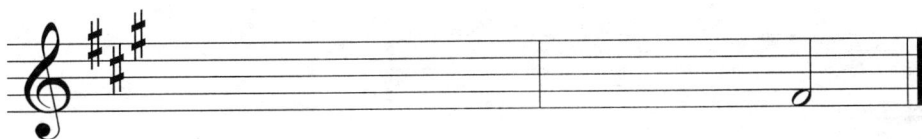

43

SECTION 4
Instructor Key

FOCUS: *Augmented fourths, beat values and divisions, simple triple meters*

PITCH *Hint: Listen for the A4.*

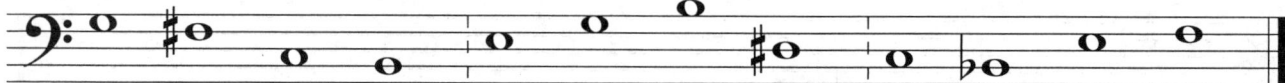

RHYTHM

MELODY

SECTION 4
Student Answer

4

FOCUS: Augmented fourths, beat values and divisions, simple triple meters

PITCH Hint: Listen for the A4.

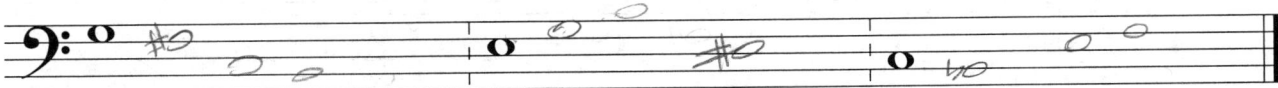

RHYTHM

MELODY

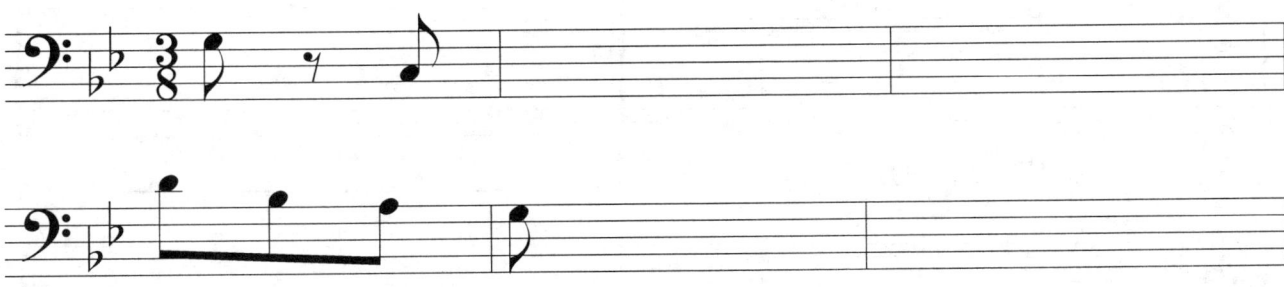

SECTION 4A
Harmony

FOCUS: *Leading tone secondary dominants of the dominant*

INSTRUCTOR KEY　　　　　**STUDENT ANSWER**

1. C: I viio6/V V I 　　C: __ __ __ __
2. C: I viio7/V V I 　　C: __ __ __ __
3. C: I I6 viio7/V V 　　C: __ __ __ __
4. C: I viio4/3 of V viio6/5 of V V 　　C: __ __ __ __
5. C: I IV viio6/V V 　　C: __ __ __ __
6. C: I viio7 viio4/3 of V V6 　　C: __ __ __ __

# SECTION 4A
Harmony

FOCUS: Leading tone secondary dominants of the dominant

SECTION 4B
Harmony

CD 23

FOCUS: *Leading tone secondary dominants of the dominant*

INSTRUCTOR KEY — **STUDENT ANSWER**

1. a: i — viio6/V — V — i || a: ___ ___ ___ ___

2. a: i — viio6/5 of V — viio7/V — V || a: ___ ___ ___ ___

3. a: i — i6/4 — viio7/V — V || a: ___ ___ ___ ___

4. a: i — i6 — viio4/3 of V — V || a: ___ ___ ___ ___

5. a: viio7/V — viio6/5 of V — V — i || a: ___ ___ ___ ___

6. a: viio6/V — V — viio7/V — V || a: ___ ___ ___ ___

SECTION 4B
Harmony

FOCUS: Leading tone secondary dominants of the dominant

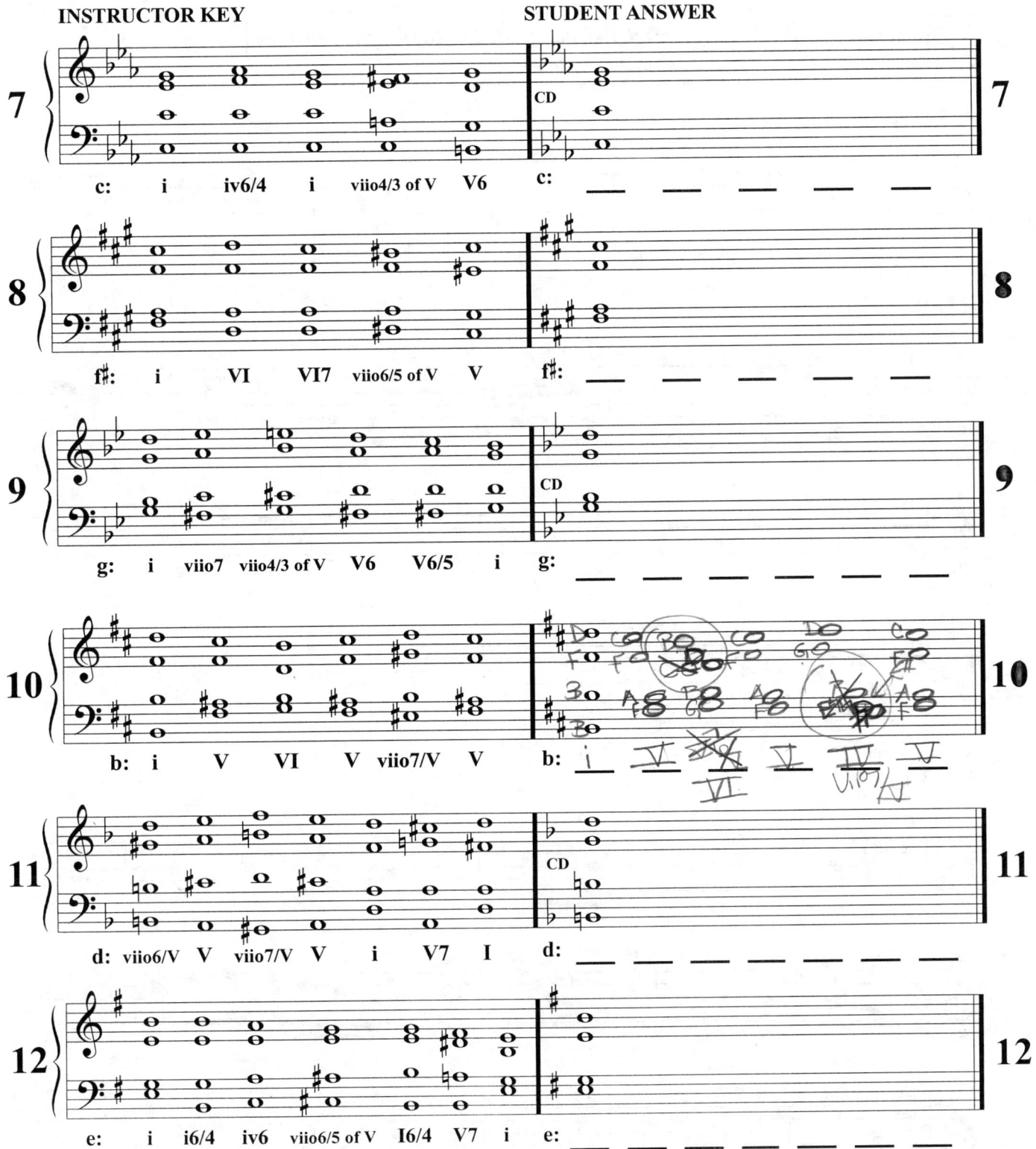

SECTION 5
Instructor Key

1 CD 25

> *FOCUS:* Diminished 5th, beat divisions and subdivisions, dotted values, syncopation, simple triple meters

PITCH   *Hint: Listen for the d5*

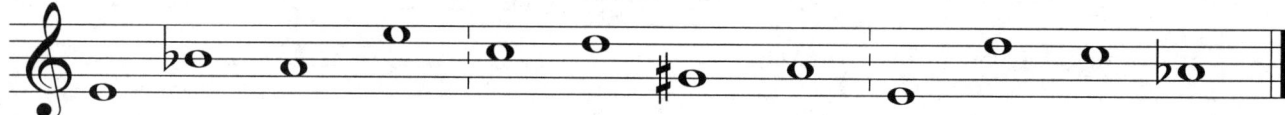

RHYTHM

MELODY

SECTION 5
Student Answer

1 CD 25

FOCUS: Diminished 5th, beat divisions and subdivisions, dotted values, syncopation, simple triple meters

PITCH *Hint: Listen for the d5*

RHYTHM

MELODY

SECTION 5
Instructor Key

2

> *FOCUS:* *Diminished 5th, beat divisions and subdivisions, dotted values, syncopation, simple triple meters*

PITCH *Hint: Listen for the d5*

RHYTHM

MELODY

SECTION 5
Student Answer

2

> *FOCUS:* Diminished 5th, beat divisions and subdivisions, dotted values, syncopation, simple triple meters

PITCH   *Hint: Listen for the d5*

RHYTHM

MELODY

SECTION 5
Instructor Key

FOCUS: Diminished 5th, beat divisions and subdivisions, dotted values, syncopation, simple triple meters

PITCH   *Hint: Listen for the d5*

RHYTHM

MELODY

SECTION 5
Student Answer

3 CD 26

FOCUS: Diminished 5th, beat divisions and subdivisions, dotted values, syncopation, simple triple meters

PITCH   *Hint: Listen for the d5*

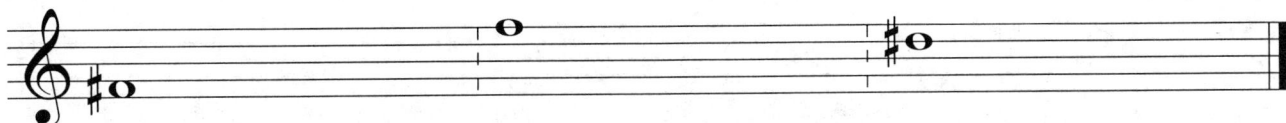

RHYTHM

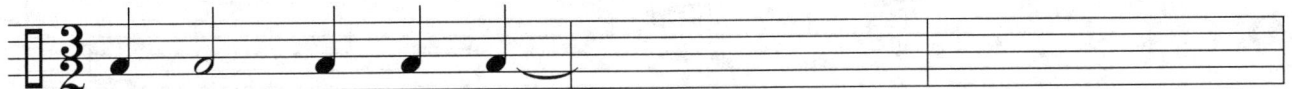

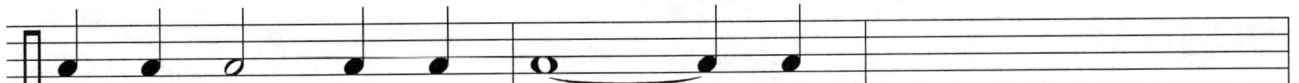

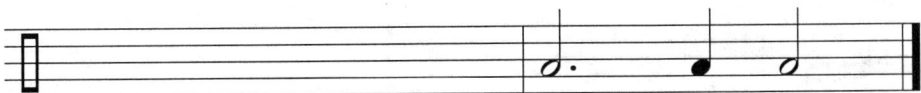

MELODY

55

SECTION 5
Instructor Key

4

> *FOCUS: Diminished 5th, beat divisions and subdivisions, dotted values, syncopation, simple triple meters*

PITCH   *Hint: Listen for the d5*

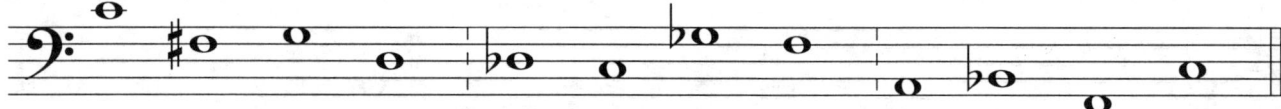

RHYTHM

MELODY

SECTION 5
Student Answer

FOCUS: Diminished 5th, beat divisions and subdivisions, dotted values, syncopation, simple triple meters

4

PITCH   *Hint: Listen for the d5*

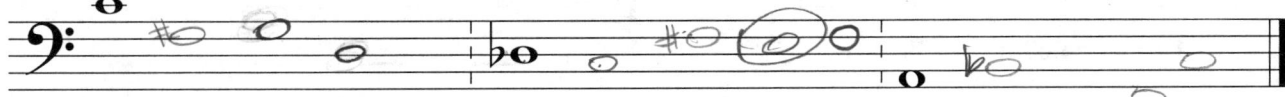

RHYTHM

MELODY

57

CD 27

FOCUS: *Leading tone secondary dominants of supertonic and subdominant*

SECTION 5A
Harmony

INSTRUCTOR KEY   **STUDENT ANSWER**

1. C: I   viio7/ii   ii   V   C: ___ ___ ___ ___

2. C: I6   viio7/IV   IV   V   C: ___ ___ ___ ___

3. C: I   viio4/3 of ii   ii6   V   C: ___ ___ ___ ___

4. C: I   viio4/3 of ii   ii6   V   C: ___ ___ ___ ___

5. C: I   V   viio6/5 of IV   IV   C: ___ ___ ___ ___

6. C: I   viio2/IV   IV6/4   I   C: ___ ___ ___ ___

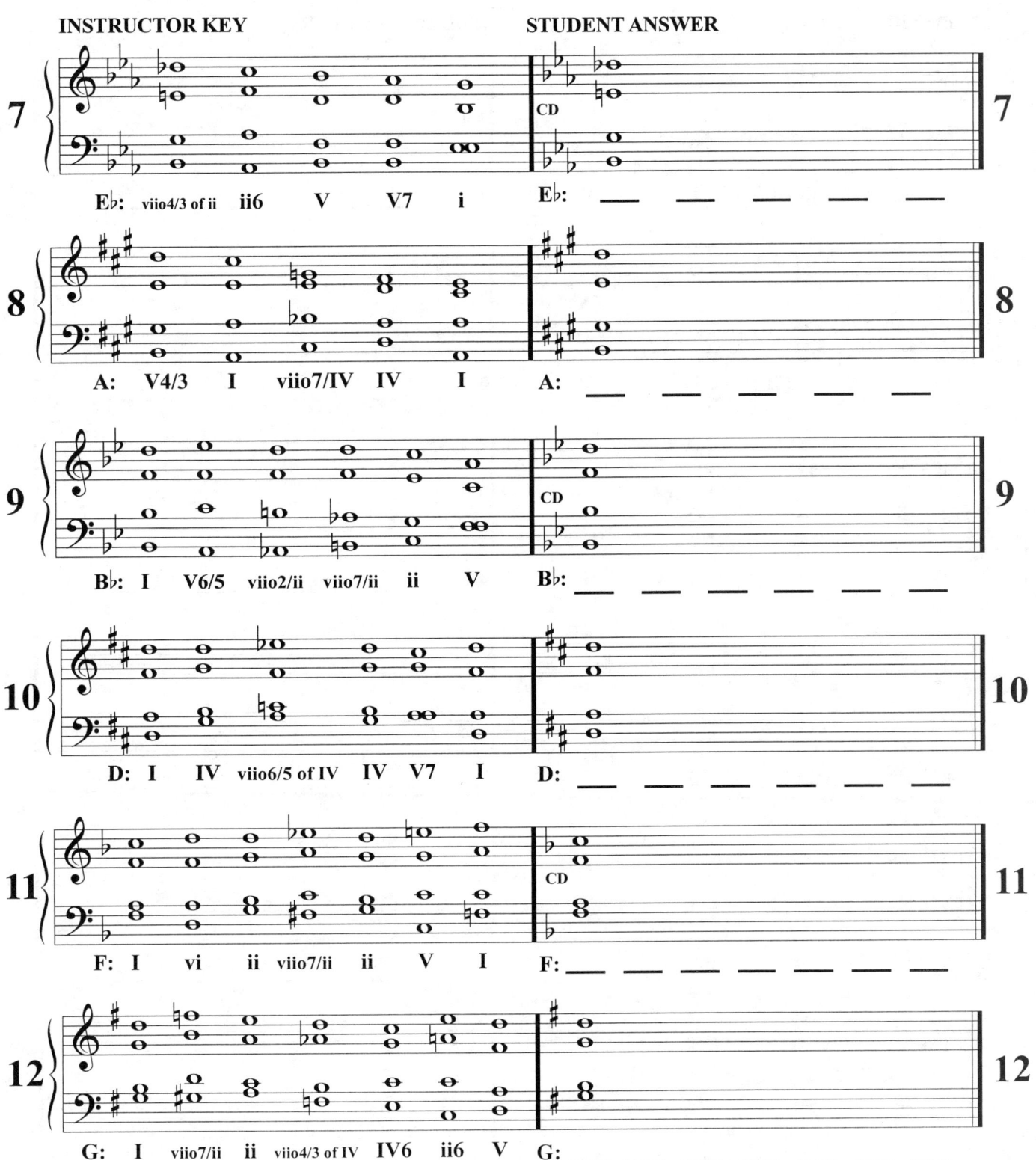

CD 29

FOCUS: *Leading tone secondary dominants of supertonic and subdominant*

SECTION 5B
Harmony

INSTRUCTOR KEY   **STUDENT ANSWER**

1. a: i — viio7/ii — ii — V   a: _ _ _ _

2. a: i6 — viio7/iv — iv — V   a: _ _ _ _

3. a: i — V — viio7/iv — iv   a: _ _ _ _

4. a: i — viio7/ii — ii — V   a: _ _ _ _

5. a: i — V6/4 — viio7/iv — iv   a: _ _ _ _

6. a: i — VI — viio4/3 of iv — iv6   a: _ _ _ _

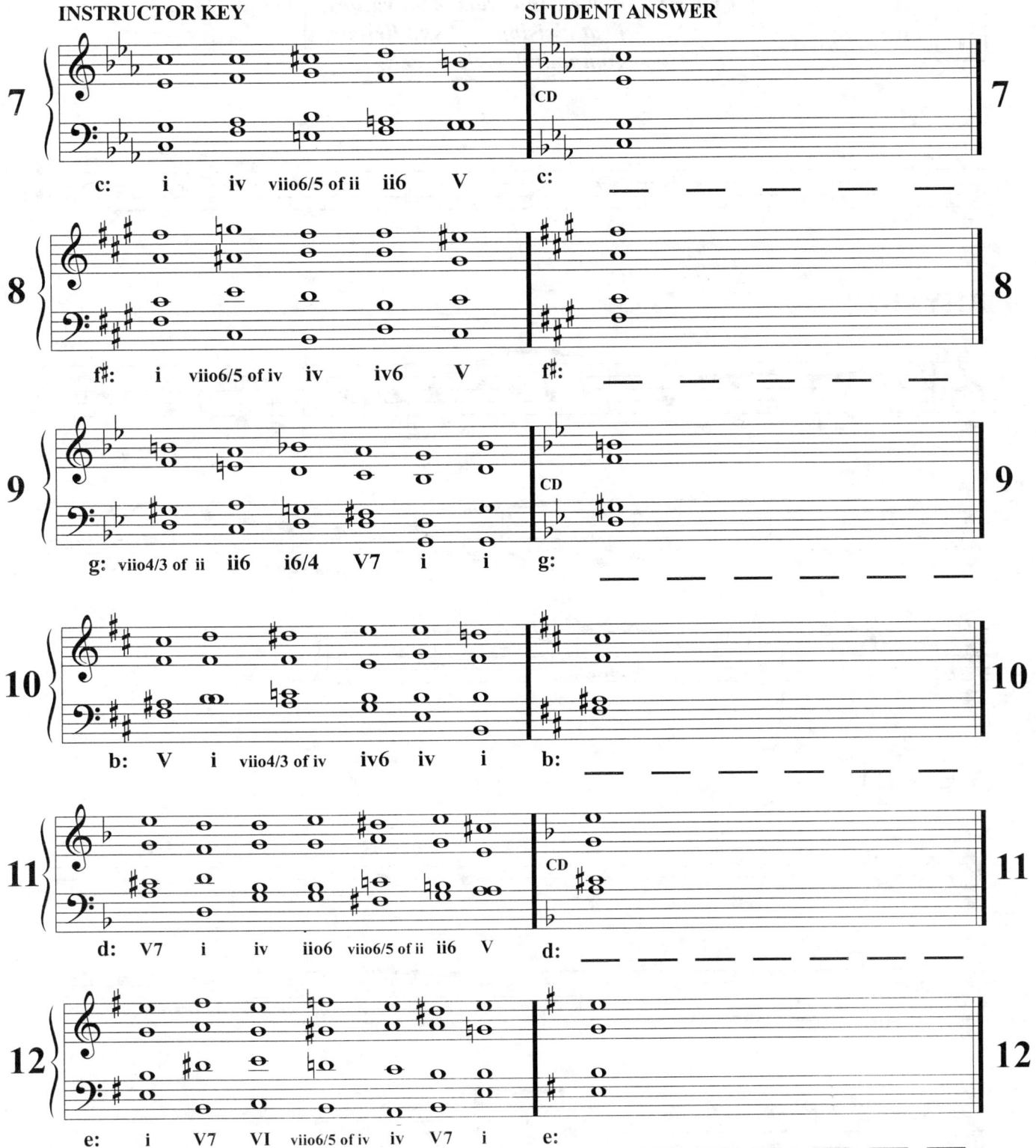

SECTION 6
Instructor Key

1 CD 31

FOCUS: Review intervals, beat values, beat division and subdivions, compound triple meters

PITCH

RHYTHM

MELODY

SECTION 6
Student Answer

1 CD 31

FOCUS: Review intervals, beat values, beat division and subdivions, compound triple meters

PITCH

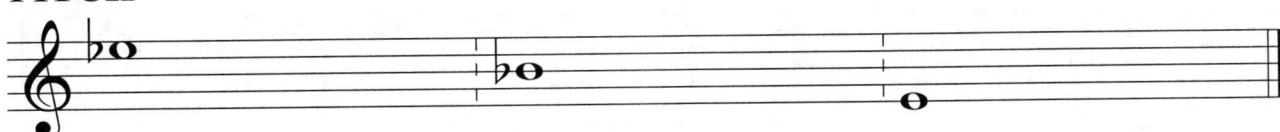

RHYTHM

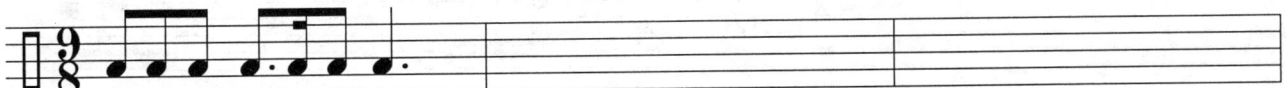

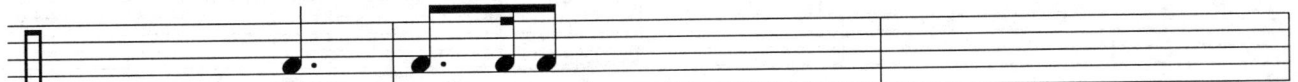

MELODY

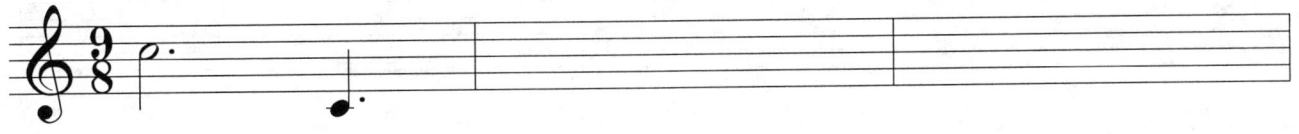

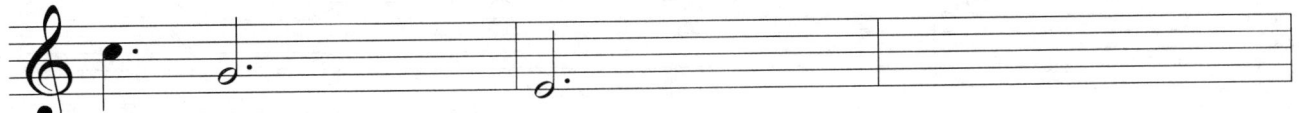

SECTION 6
Instructor Key

> *FOCUS:* Review intervals, beat values, beat division and subdivions, compound triple meters

2

PITCH

RHYTHM

MELODY

SECTION 6
Student Answer

FOCUS: Review intervals, beat values, beat division and subdivions, compound triple meters

2

PITCH

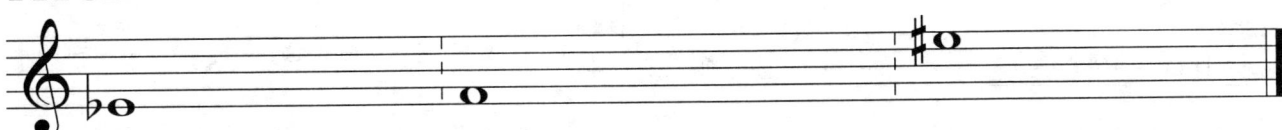

RHYTHM

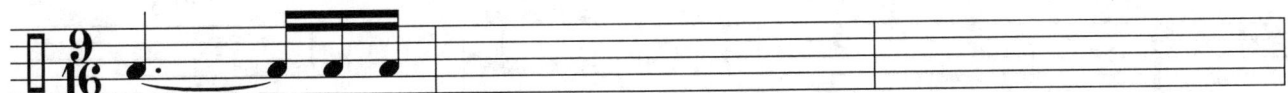

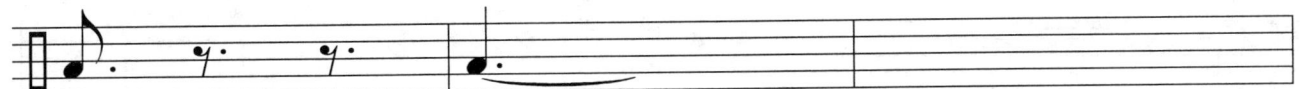

MELODY

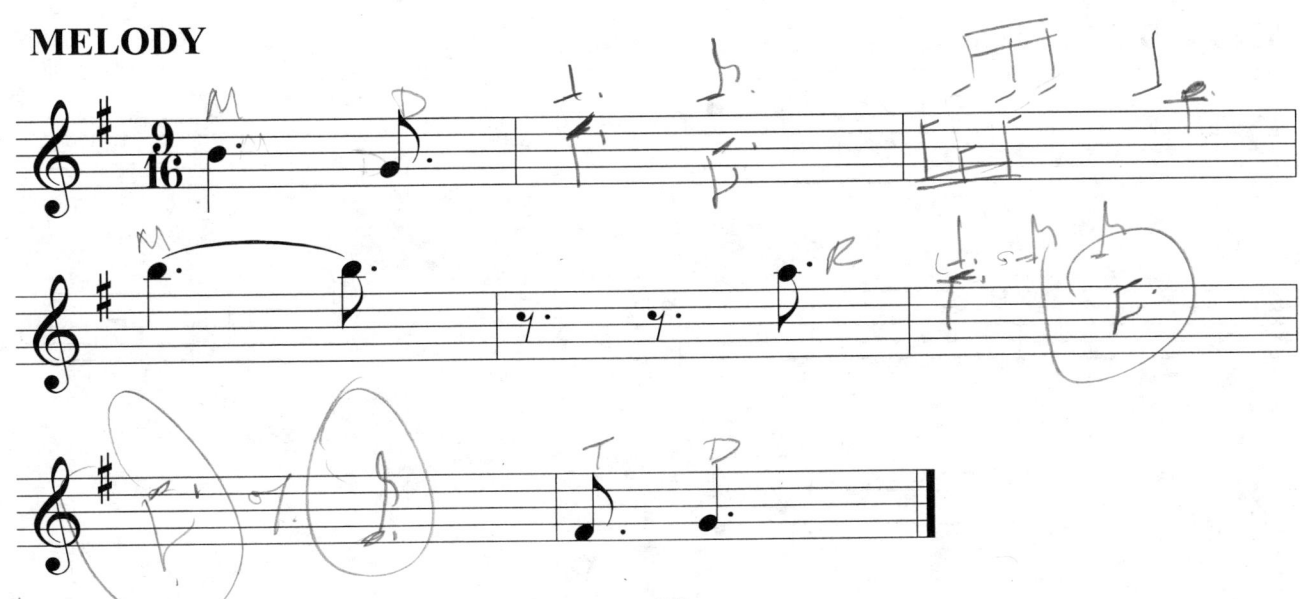

SECTION 6
Instructor Key

3 CD 32

FOCUS: Review intervals, beat values, beat division and subdivions, compound triple meters

PITCH

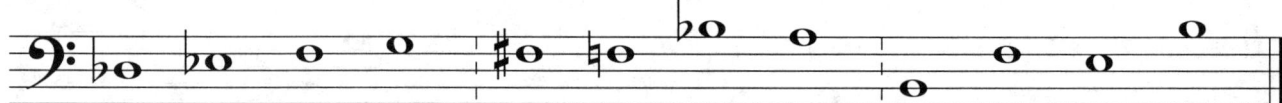

RHYTHM

MELODY

SECTION 6
Student Answer

FOCUS: Review intervals, beat values, beat division and subdivions, compound triple meters

3 CD 32

PITCH

RHYTHM

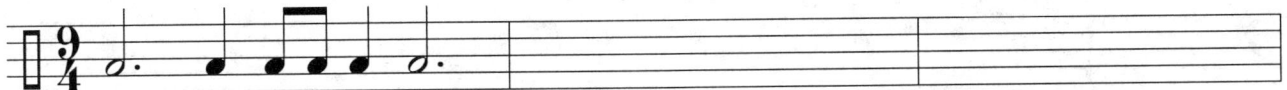

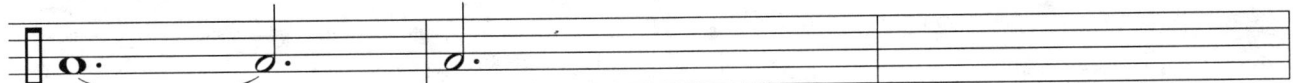

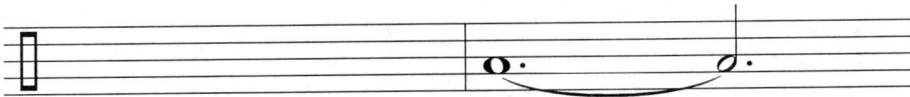

MELODY

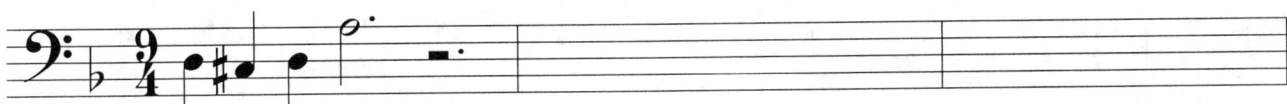

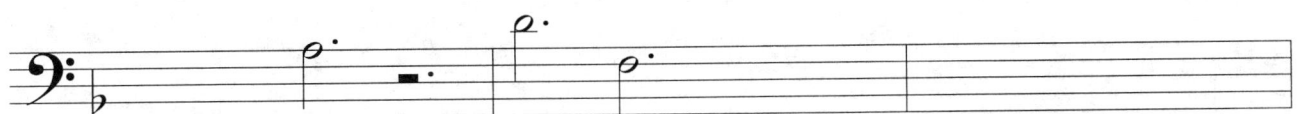

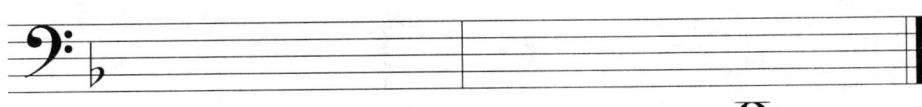

SECTION 6
Instructor Key

> *FOCUS:* Review intervals, beat values, beat division and subdivions, compound triple meters

4

PITCH

RHYTHM

MELODY

SECTION 6
Student Answer

FOCUS: Review intervals, beat values, beat division and subdivions, compound triple meters

4

PITCH

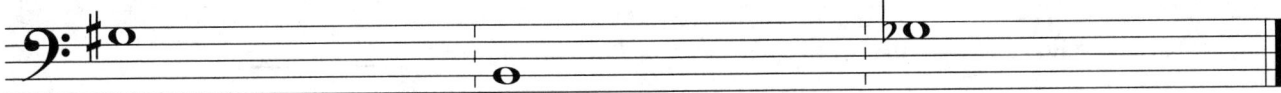

RHYTHM

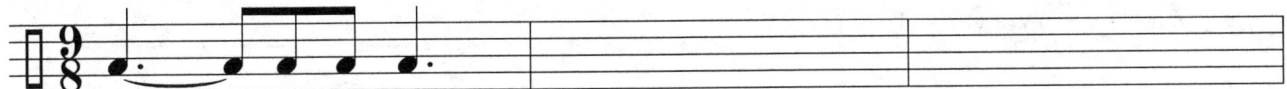

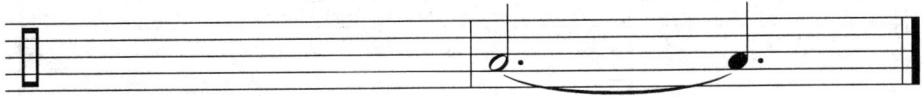

MELODY

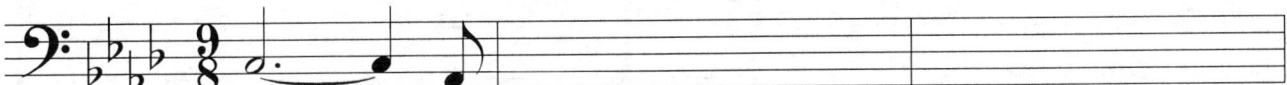

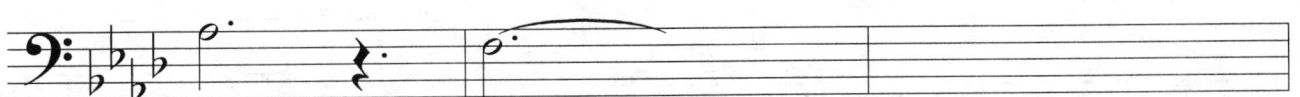

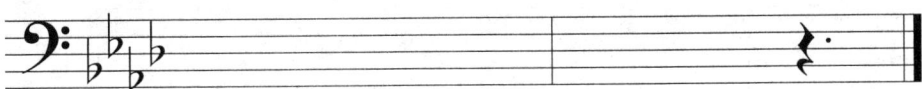

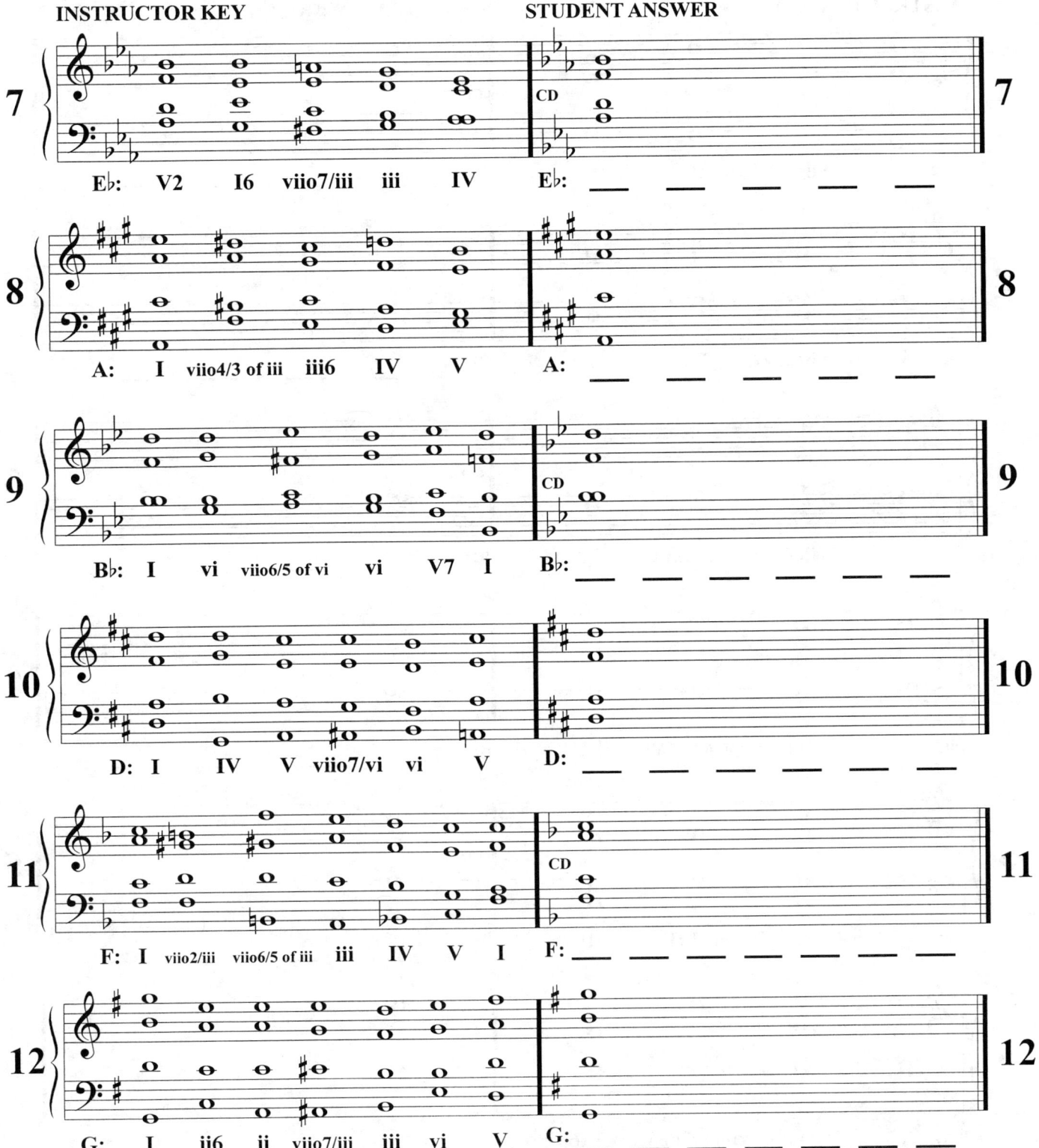

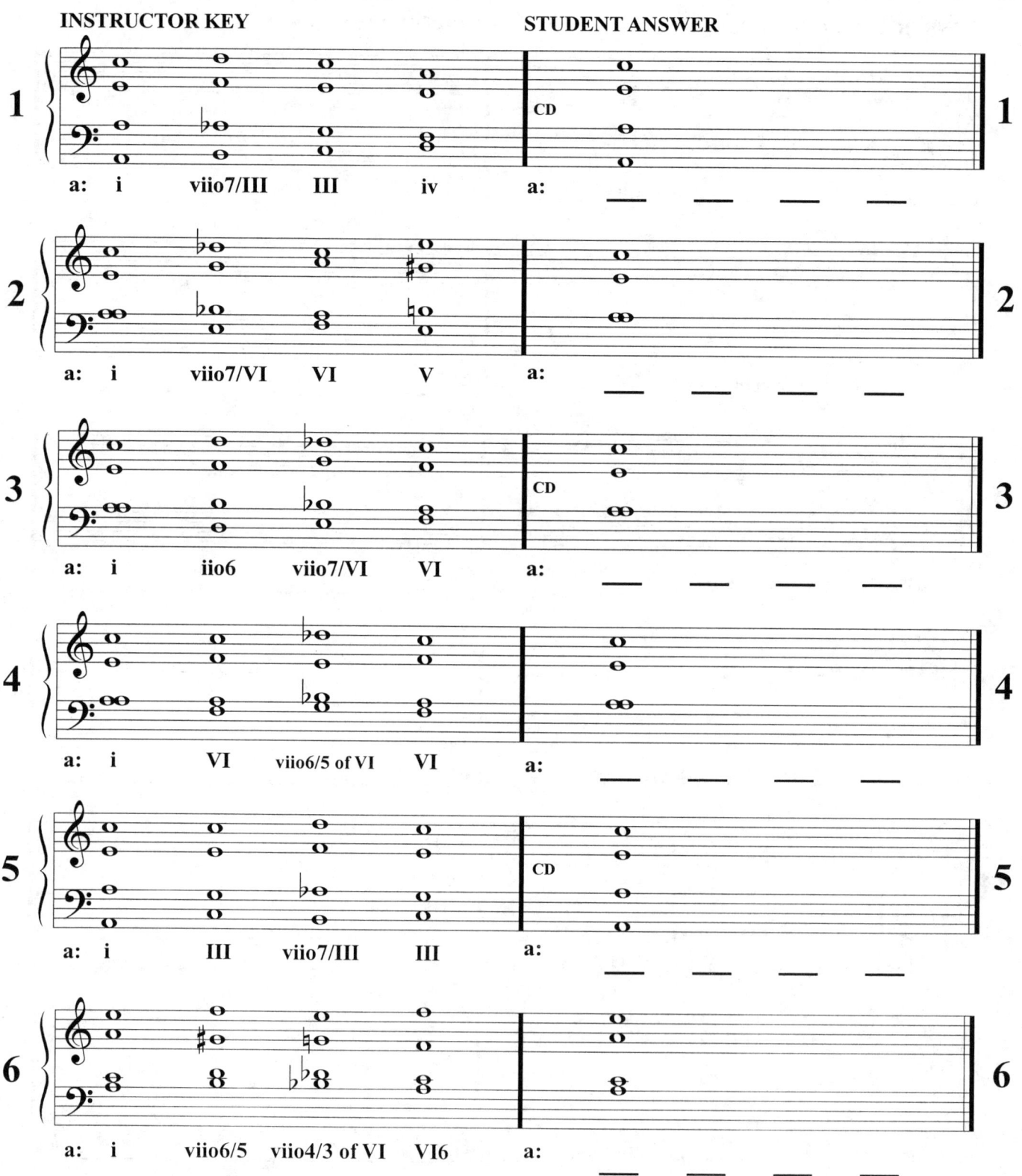

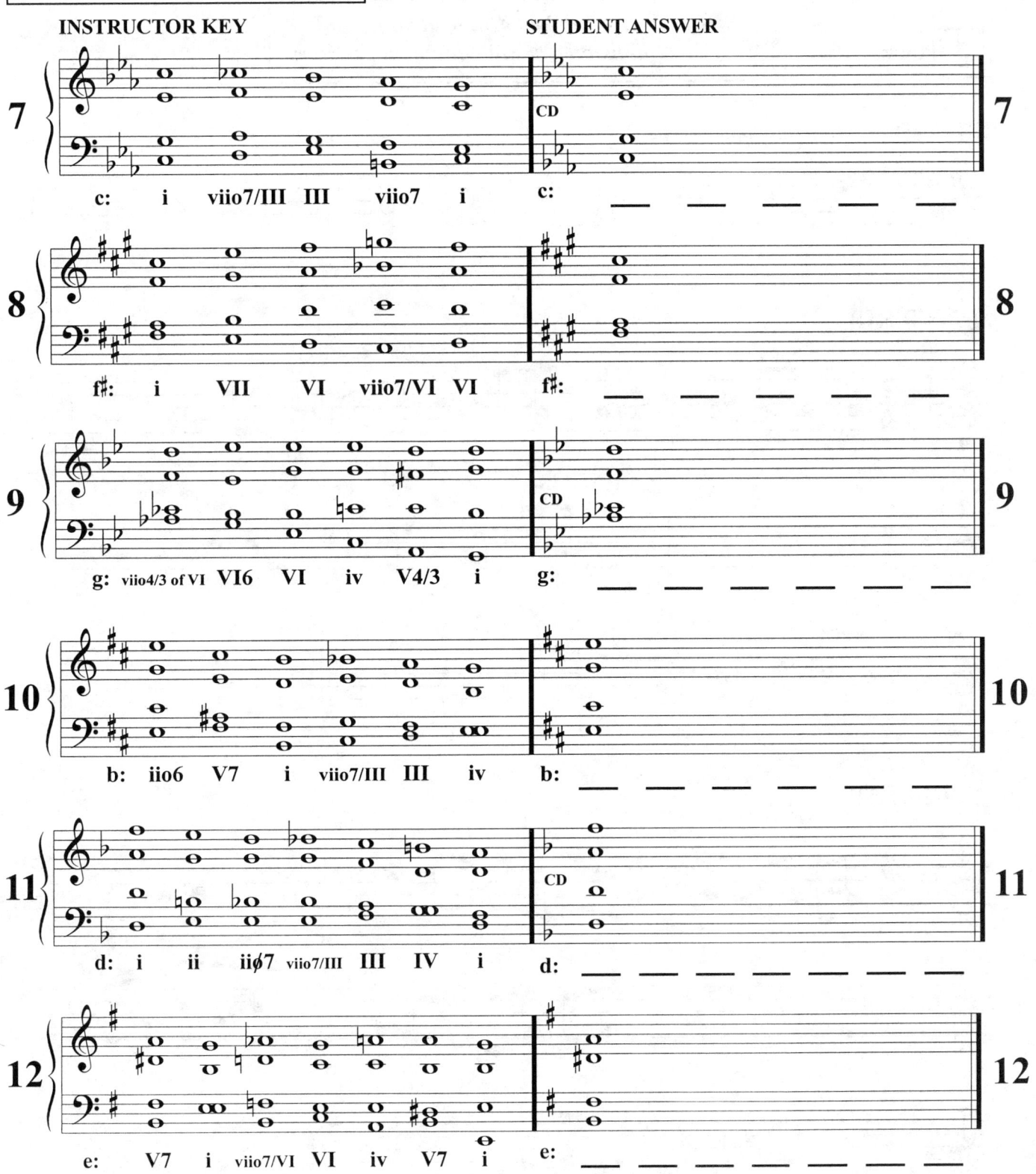

SECTION 7
Instructor Key

1 CD 37

FOCUS: Diminished 4th, beat values and divisions, simple quadruple meters

PITCH   *Hint: Listen for the d4*

RHYTHM

MELODY

SECTION 7
Student Answer

FOCUS: Diminished 4th, beat values and divisions, simple quadruple meters

SECTION 7
Instructor Key

2

FOCUS: Diminished 4th, beat values and divisions, simple quadruple meters

PITCH

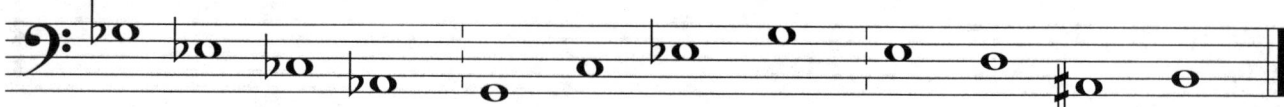

RHYTHM

MELODY

SECTION 7
Student Answer

FOCUS: Diminished 4th, beat values and divisions, simple quadruple meters

2

PITCH

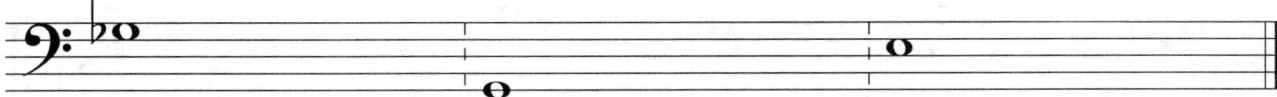

RHYTHM

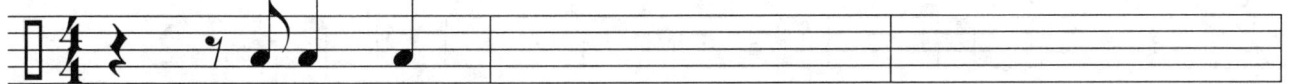

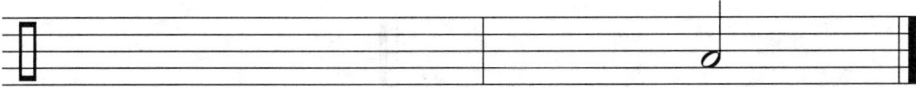

MELODY

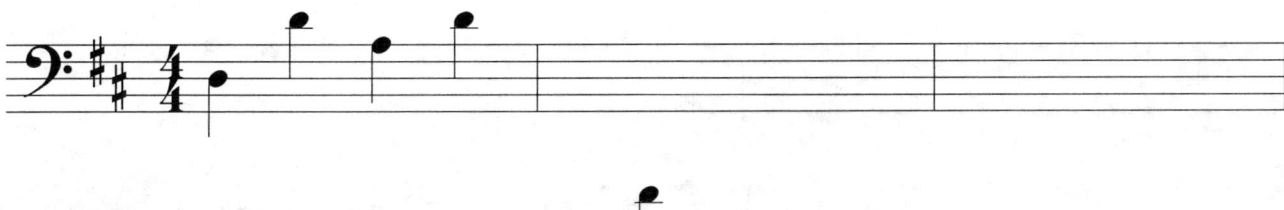

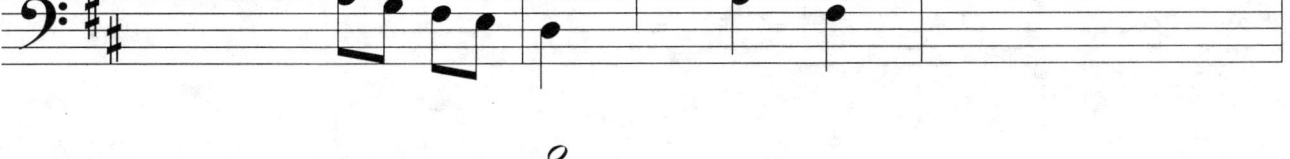

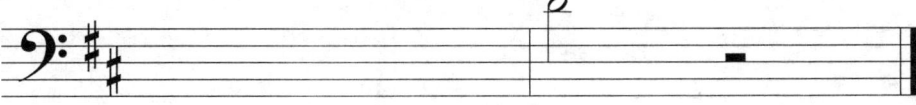

SECTION 7
Instructor Key

3 CD 38

FOCUS: Diminished 4th, beat values and divisions, simple quadruple meters

PITCH

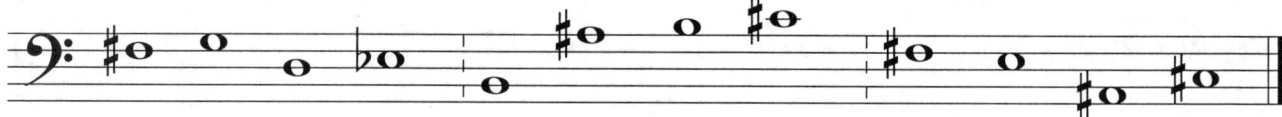

RHYTHM

MELODY

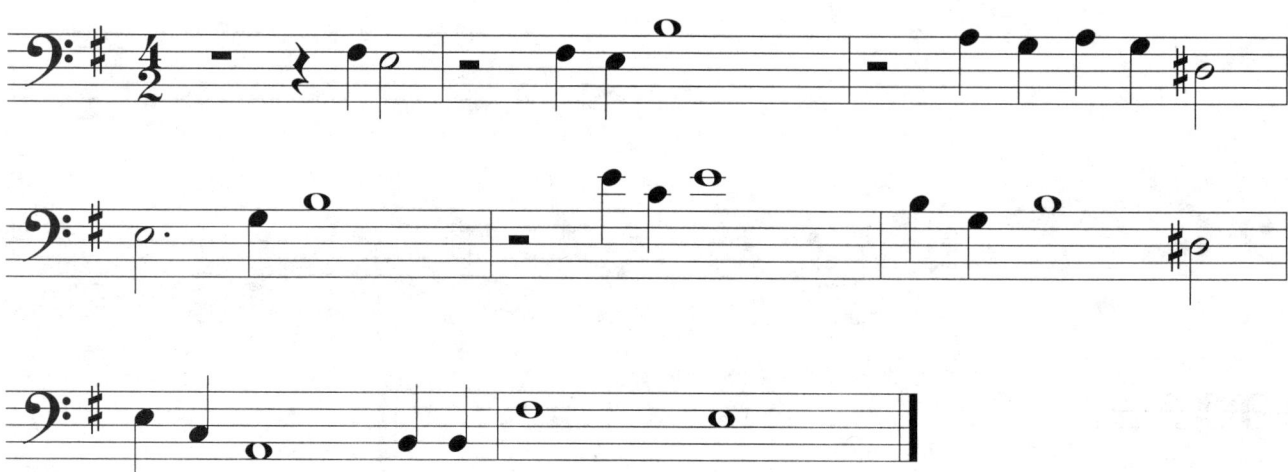

SECTION 7
Student Answer

FOCUS: Diminished 4th, beat values and divisions, simple quadruple meters

3 CD 38

PITCH

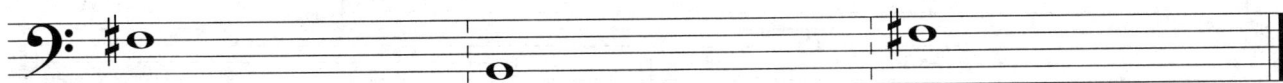

RHYTHM

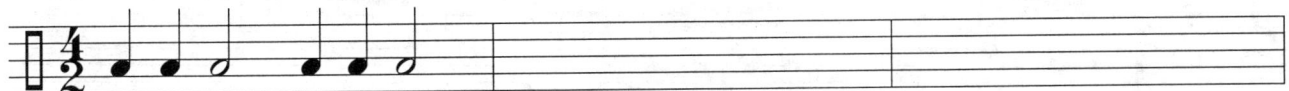

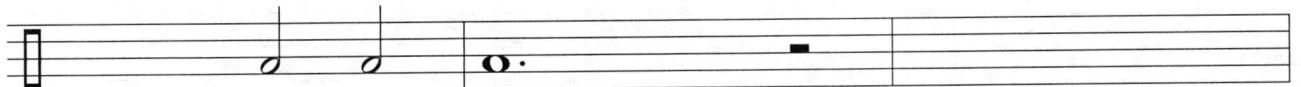

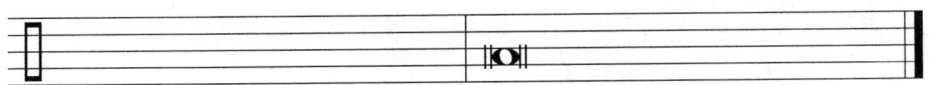

MELODY

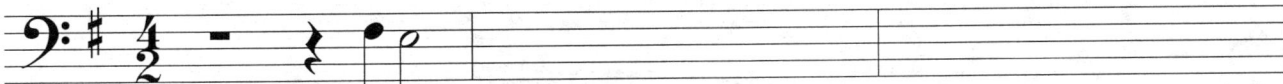

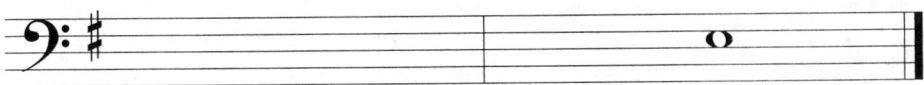

SECTION 7
Instructor Key

4

FOCUS: Diminished 4th, beat values and divisions, simple quadruple meters

PITCH

RHYTHM

MELODY

SECTION 7
Student Answer

FOCUS: Diminished 4th, beat values and divisions, simple quadruple meters

4

PITCH

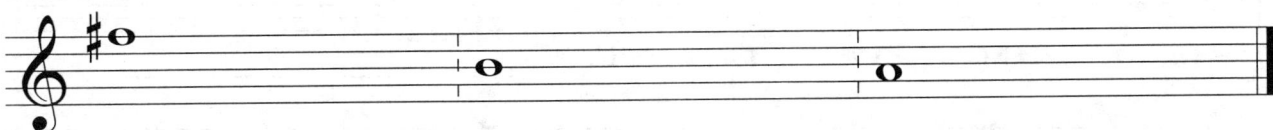

RHYTHM

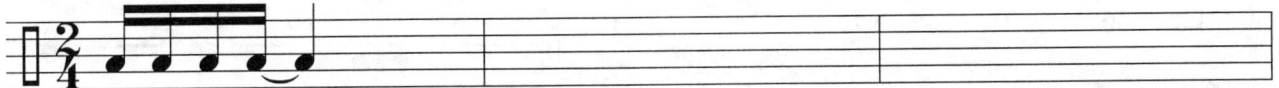

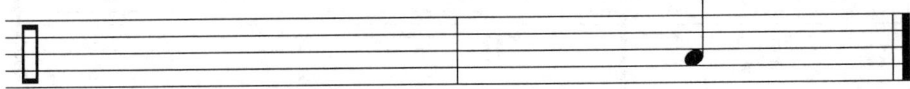

MELODY

SECTION 7A
Harmony

FOCUS: *Neapolitan sixth*

INSTRUCTOR KEY   **STUDENT ANSWER**

1. C: IV   N6   V7   I   C: __ __ __ __

2. C: I6   N6   V7   I   C: __ __ __ __

3. C: I   IV   N6   V   C: __ __ __ __

4. C: ii6   N6   I6/4   V   C: __ __ __ __

5. C: N6   V7   V6/5   I   C: __ __ __ __

6. C: I   VI   N6   V   C: __ __ __ __

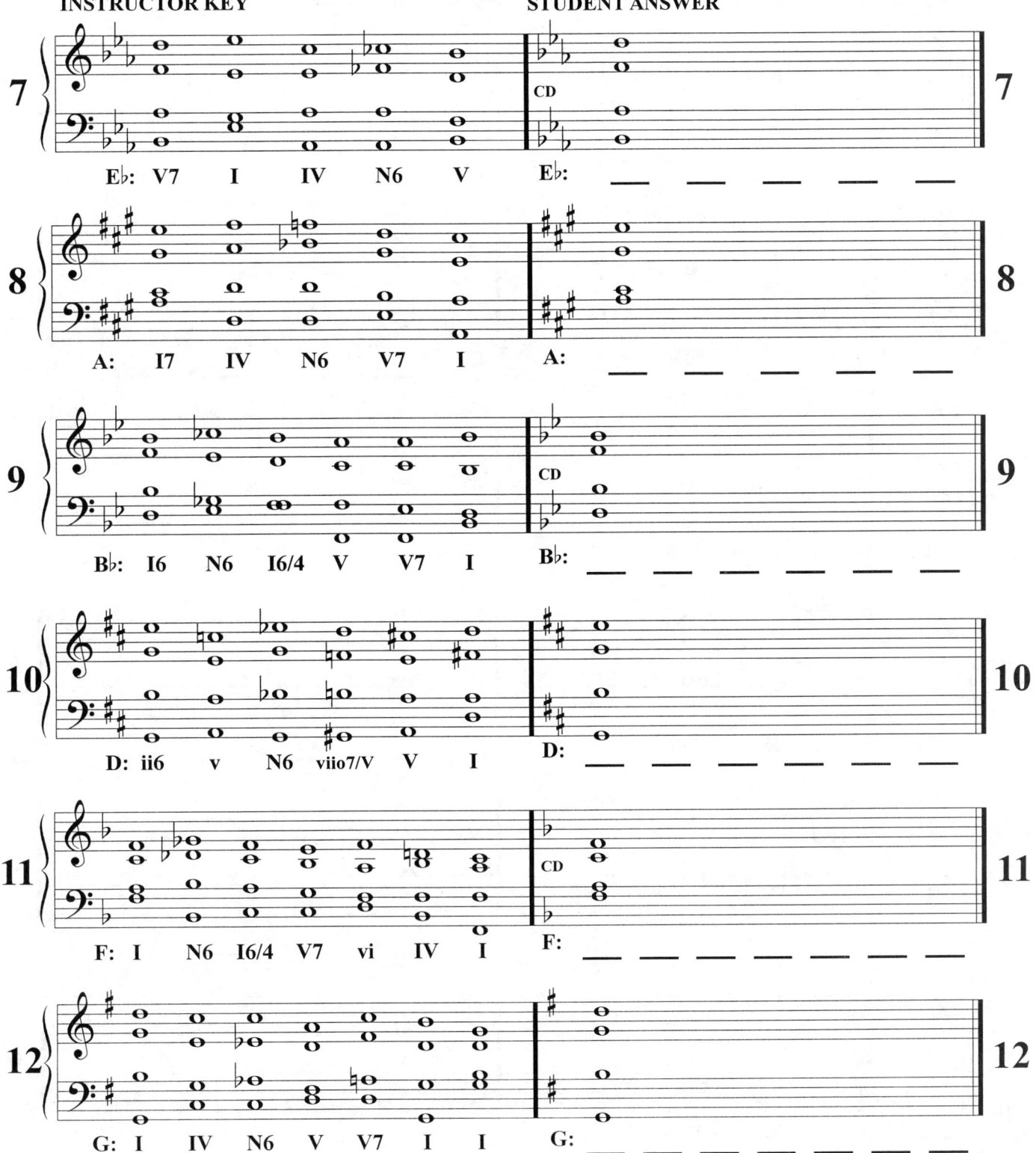

SECTION 7B
Harmony

FOCUS: Neapolitan sixth

INSTRUCTOR KEY / STUDENT ANSWER

1. a: i — N6 — V — V
2. a: i6 — N6 — i6/4 — V
3. a: iv — N6 — i6/4 — V
4. a: i — i6 — N6 — V7
5. a: N6 — V — V7 — i
6. a: iv — N6 — i6/4 — V

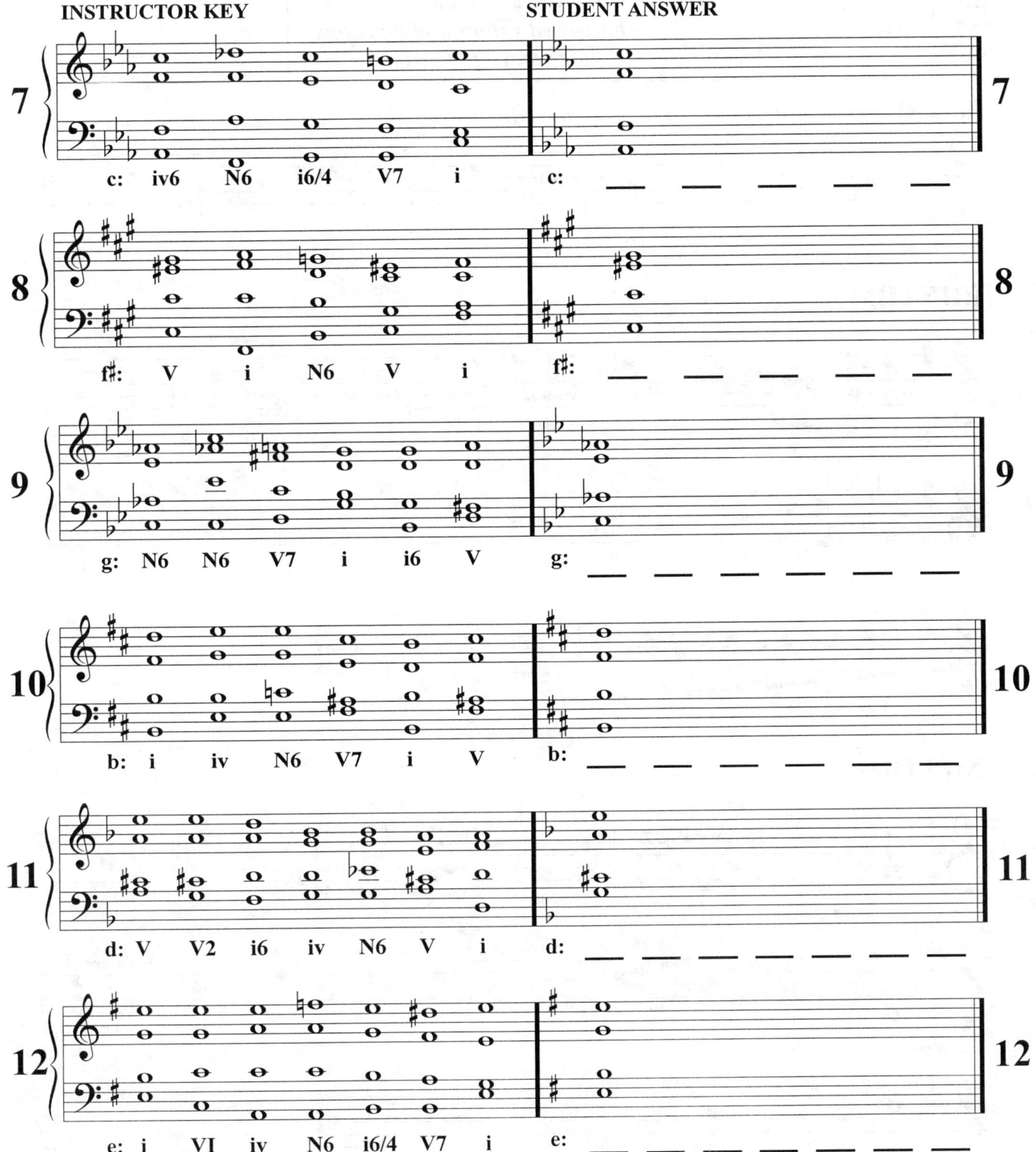

SECTION 8
Instructor Key

1 CD 43

> *FOCUS:* **Diminished 7th, dotted values, borrowed values and divisions, simple quadruple meters**

PITCH   *Hint: Listen for the diminished 7th*

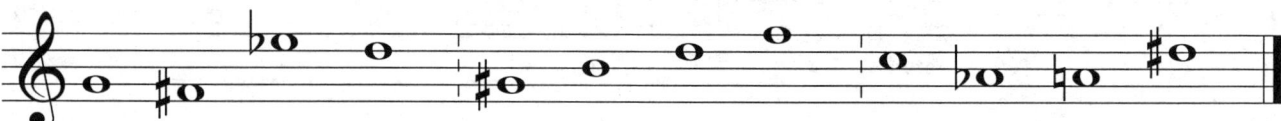

RHYTHM

MELODY

SECTION 8
Student Answer

> *FOCUS: Diminished 7th, dotted values, borrowed values and divisions, simple quadruple meters*

1 CD 43

PITCH   *Hint: Listen for the diminished 7th*

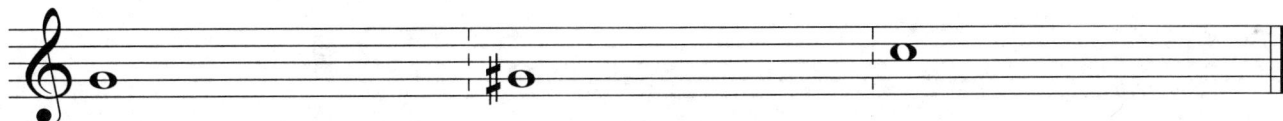

RHYTHM

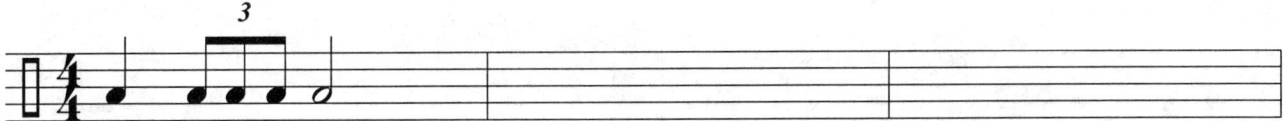

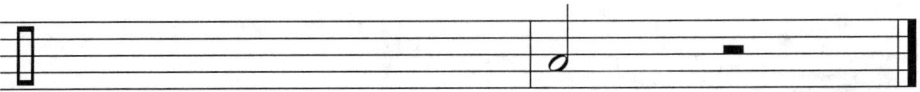

MELODY

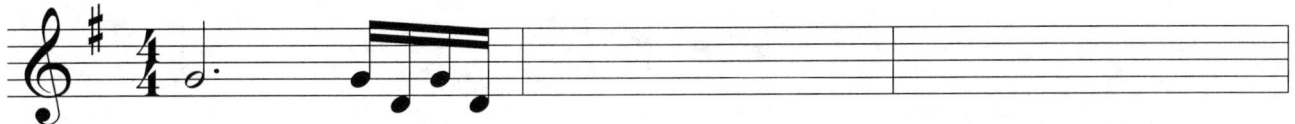

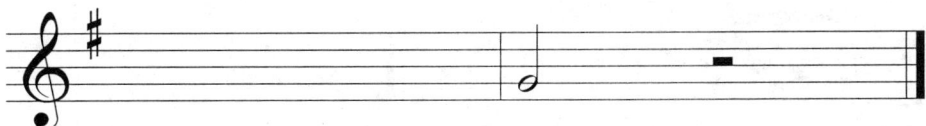

SECTION 8
Instructor Key

FOCUS: *Diminished 7th, dotted values, borrowed values and divisions, simple quadruple meters*

2

PITCH   *Hint: Listen for the diminished 7th*

RHYTHM

MELODY

SECTION 8
Student Answer

> *FOCUS: Diminished 7th, dotted values, borrowed values and divisions, simple quadruple meters*

2

PITCH *Hint: Listen for the diminished 7th*

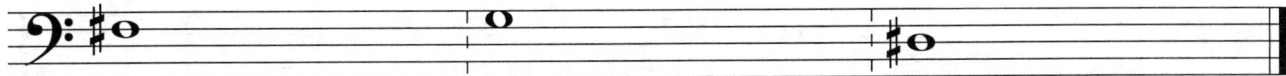

RHYTHM

MELODY

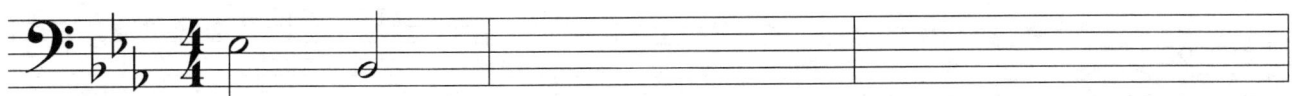

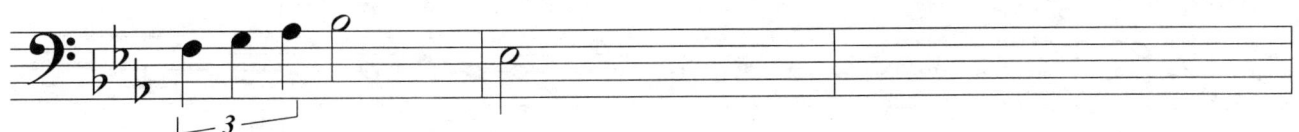

SECTION 8
Instructor Key

> *FOCUS:* Diminished 7th, dotted values, borrowed values and divisions, simple quadruple meters

3 CD 44

PITCH *Hint: Listen for the diminished 7th*

RHYTHM

MELODY

SECTION 8
Student Answer

> *FOCUS: Diminished 7th, dotted values, borrowed values and divisions, simple quadruple meters*

3 CD 44

PITCH Hint: Listen for the diminished 7th

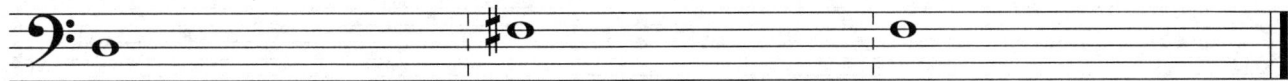

RHYTHM

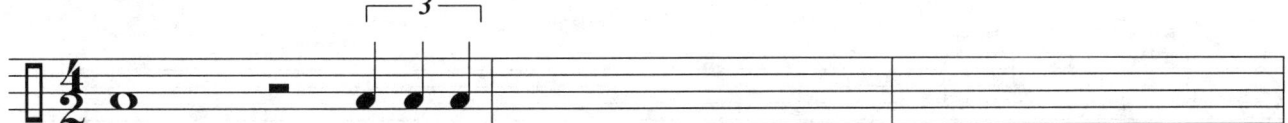

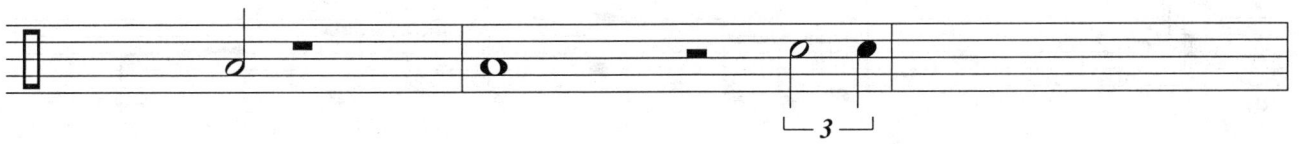

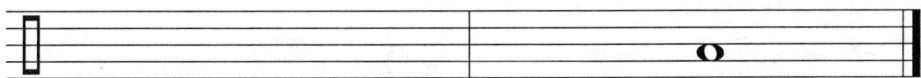

MELODY

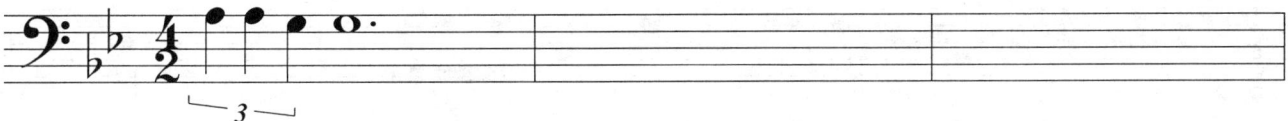

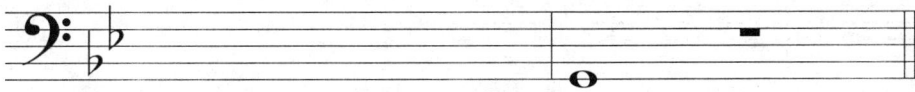

SECTION 8
Instructor Key

4

> *FOCUS: Diminished 7th, dotted values, borrowed values and divisions, simple quadruple meters*

PITCH Hint: *Listen for the diminished 7th*

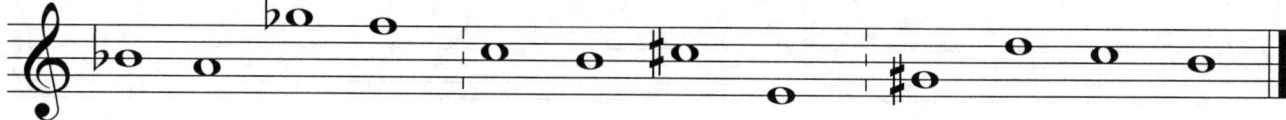

RHYTHM

MELODY

SECTION 8
Student Answer

> *FOCUS: Diminished 7th, dotted values, borrowed values and divisions, simple quadruple meters*

4

PITCH *Hint: Listen for the diminished 7th*

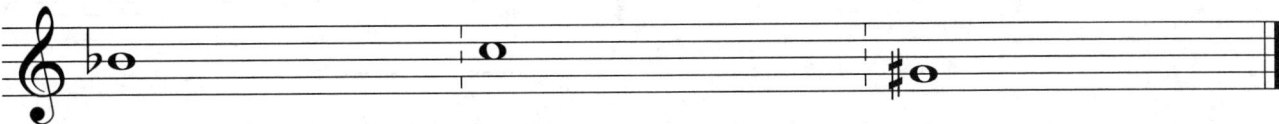

RHYTHM

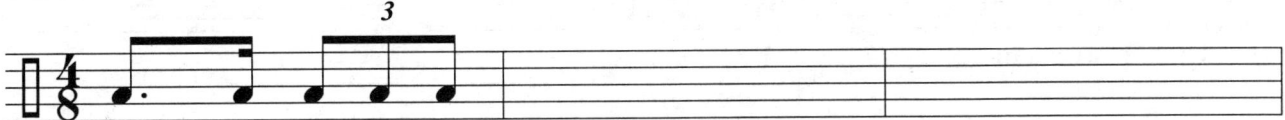

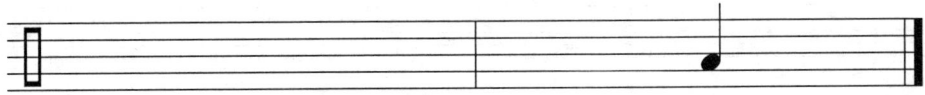

MELODY

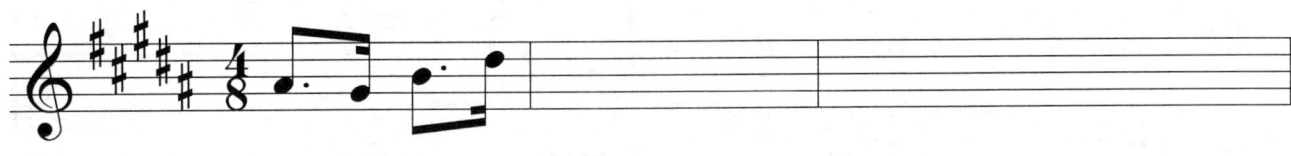

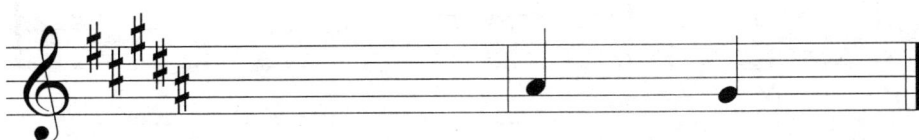

SECTION 8A
Harmony

FOCUS: *Italian sixth*

INSTRUCTOR KEY   **STUDENT ANSWER**

1. C: I — It6 — V — I   C: ___ ___ ___ ___
2. C: I — It6 — V7 — I   C: ___ ___ ___ ___
3. C: I — vi — It6 — V   C: ___ ___ ___ ___
4. C: I — It6 — V — V7   C: ___ ___ ___ ___
5. C: It6 — V — V6/5 — I   C: ___ ___ ___ ___
6. C: I — IV6 — It6 — V   C: ___ ___ ___ ___

SECTION 8A
Harmony

FOCUS: Italian sixth

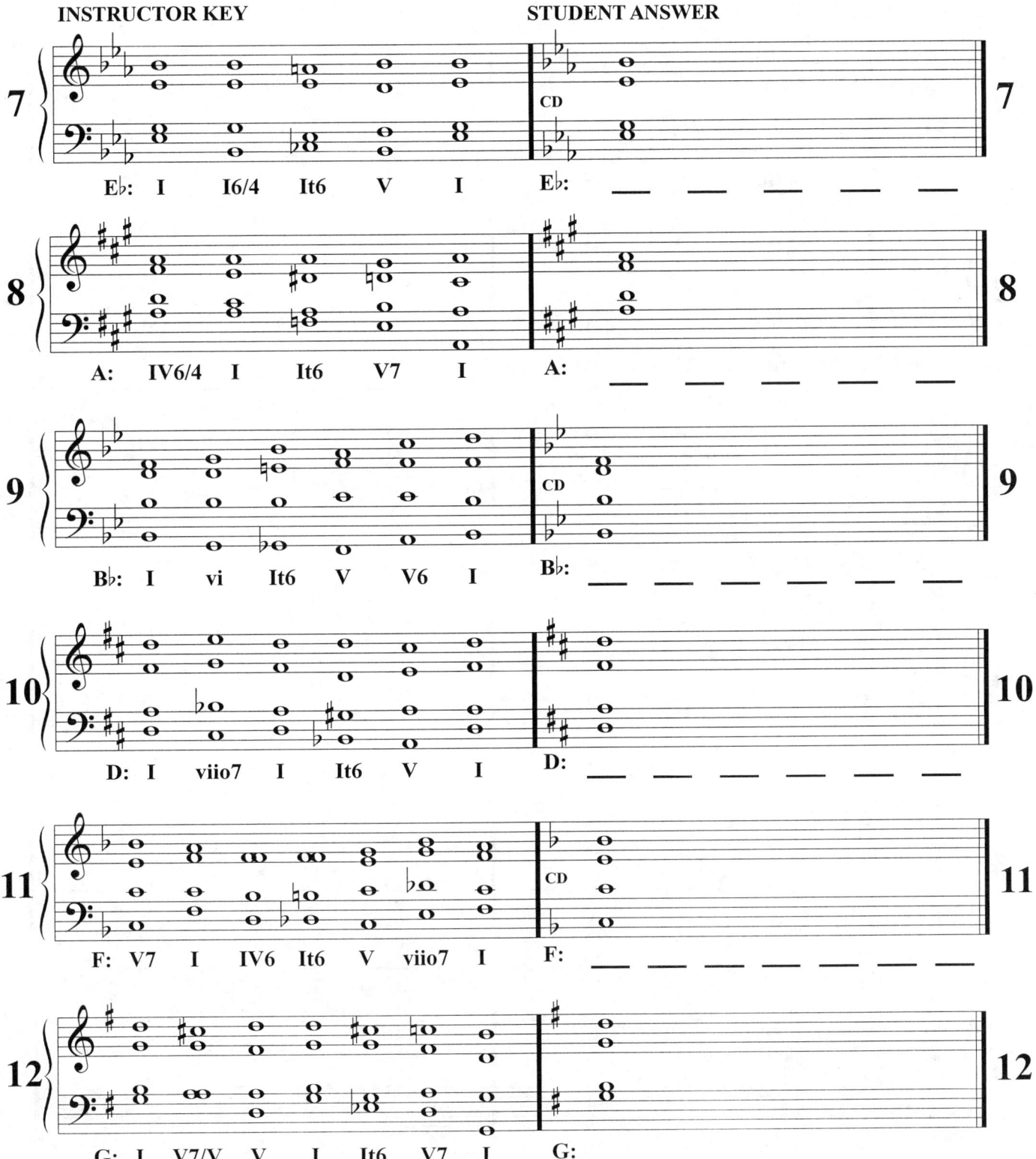

CD 47

SECTION 8B
Harmony

FOCUS: *Italian sixth*

INSTRUCTOR KEY — STUDENT ANSWER

1. a: i It6 V V — a:
2. a: i It6 V V7 — a:
3. a: i VI7 It6 V — a:
4. a: It6 V V7 i — a:
5. a: V7 i It6 V — a:
6. a: i It6 V7 VI — a:

SECTION 9
Instructor Key

1 CD 49

FOCUS: Augmented 6th, beat values, divisions, borrowed divisions, compound quadruple meters

PITCH   *Hint: Listen for the A6*

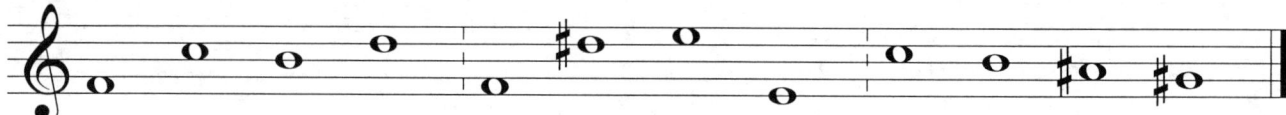

RHYTHM

MELODY

SECTION 9
Student Answer

1 CD 49

FOCUS: Augmented 6th, beat values, divisions, borrowed divisions, compound quadruple meters

PITCH   *Hint: Listen for the A6*

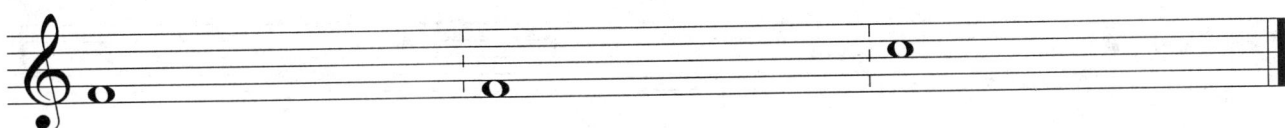

RHYTHM

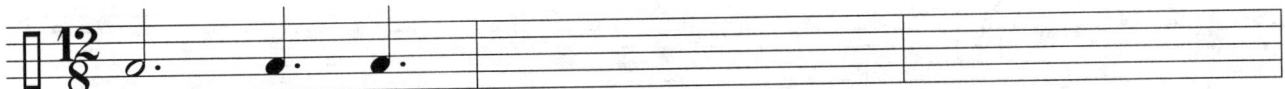

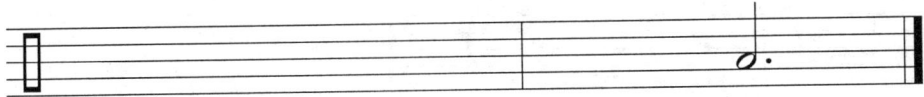

MELODY

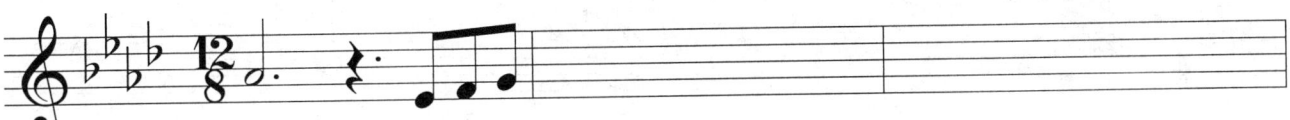

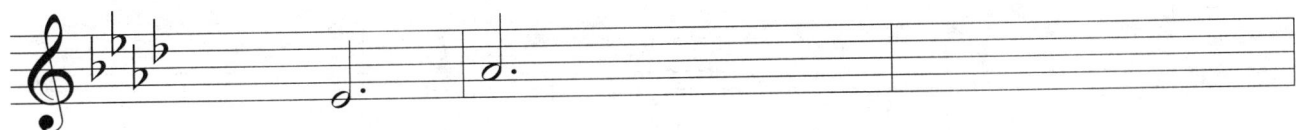

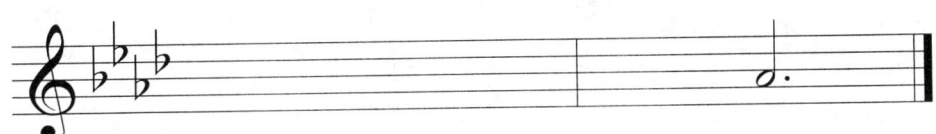

SECTION 9
Instructor Key

> *FOCUS: Augmented 6th, beat values, divisions, borrowed divisions, compound quadruple meters*

2

PITCH *Hint: Listen for the A6*

RHYTHM

MELODY

SECTION 9
Student Answer

> FOCUS: *Augmented 6th, beat values, divisions, borrowed divisions, compound quadruple meters*

2

PITCH   Hint: Listen for the A6

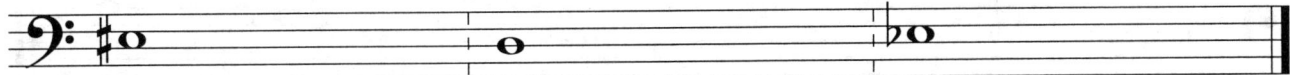

RHYTHM

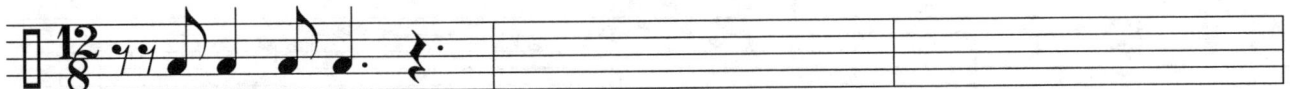

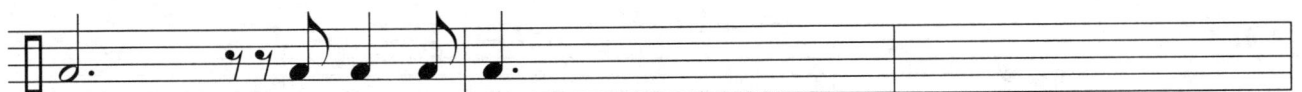

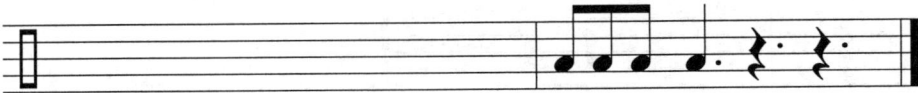

MELODY

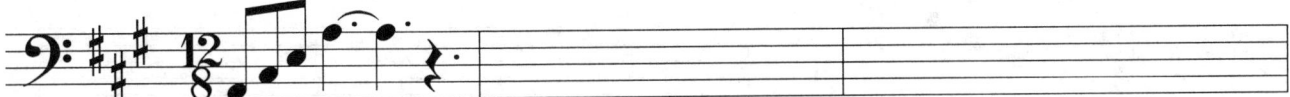

101

SECTION 9
Instructor Key

> *FOCUS:* *Augmented 6th, beat values, divisions, borrowed divisions, compound quadruple meters*

3 CD 50

PITCH   *Hint: Listen for the A6*

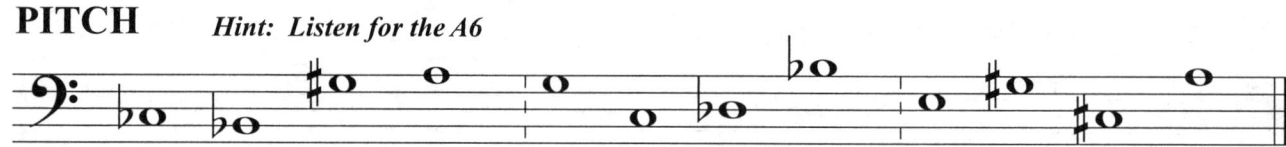

RHYTHM

MELODY

102

SECTION 9
Student Answer

> **FOCUS:** *Augmented 6th, beat values, divisions, borrowed divisions, compound quadruple meters*

3 CD 50

PITCH   Hint: Listen for the A6

RHYTHM

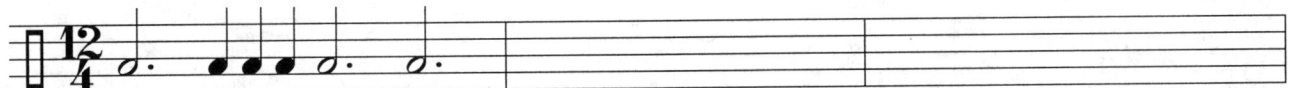

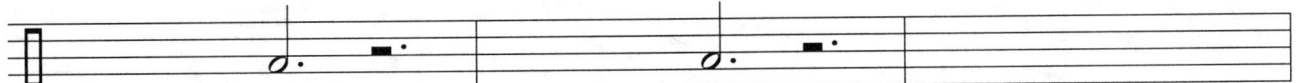

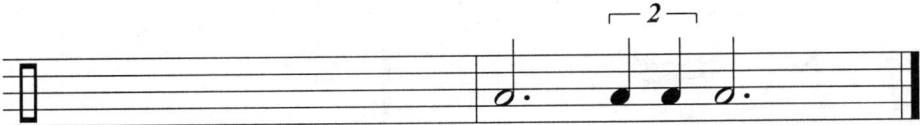

MELODY

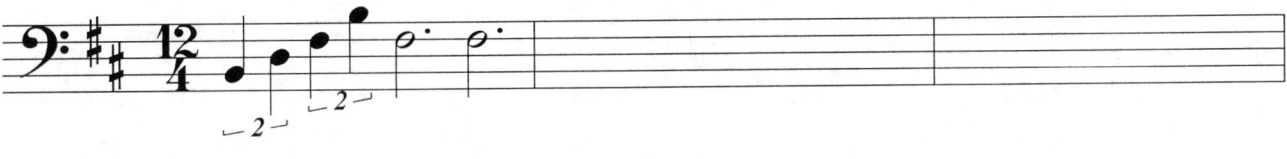

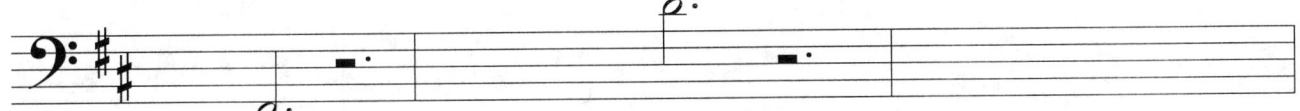

SECTION 9
Instructor Key

> *FOCUS:* **Augmented 6th, beat values, divisions, borrowed divisions, compound quadruple meters**

4

PITCH   Hint: Listen for the A6

RHYTHM

MELODY

SECTION 9
Student Answer

FOCUS: Augmented 6th, beat values, divisions, borrowed divisions, compound quadruple meters

4

PITCH *Hint: Listen for the A6*

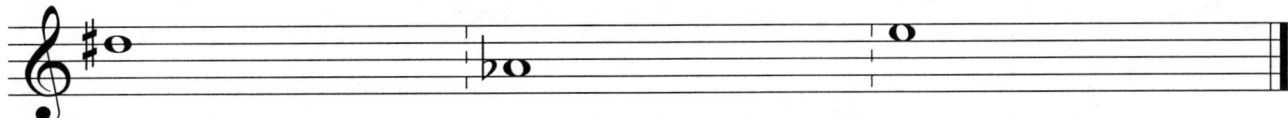

RHYTHM

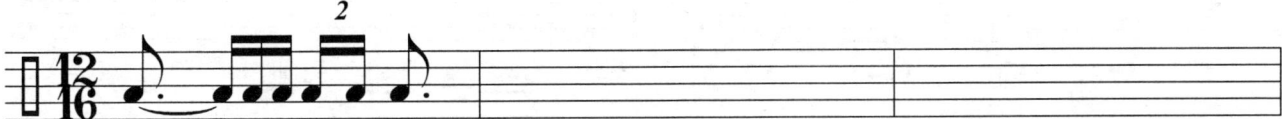

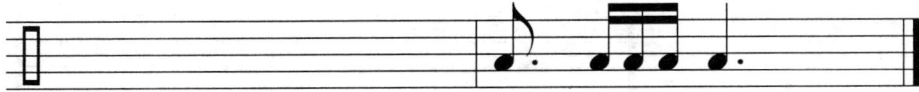

MELODY

SECTION 9A
Harmony

FOCUS: *French sixth*

INSTRUCTOR KEY   **STUDENT ANSWER**

1. C: I — F6 — V — I
2. C: I — F6 — I6/4 — V7
3. C: I — F6 — I6/4 — V7
4. C: ii4/3 — F6 — I6/4 — V7
5. C: I — F6 — F6 — I6/4
6. C: V7 — I — F6 — V

SECTION 9A
Harmony

FOCUS: *French sixth*

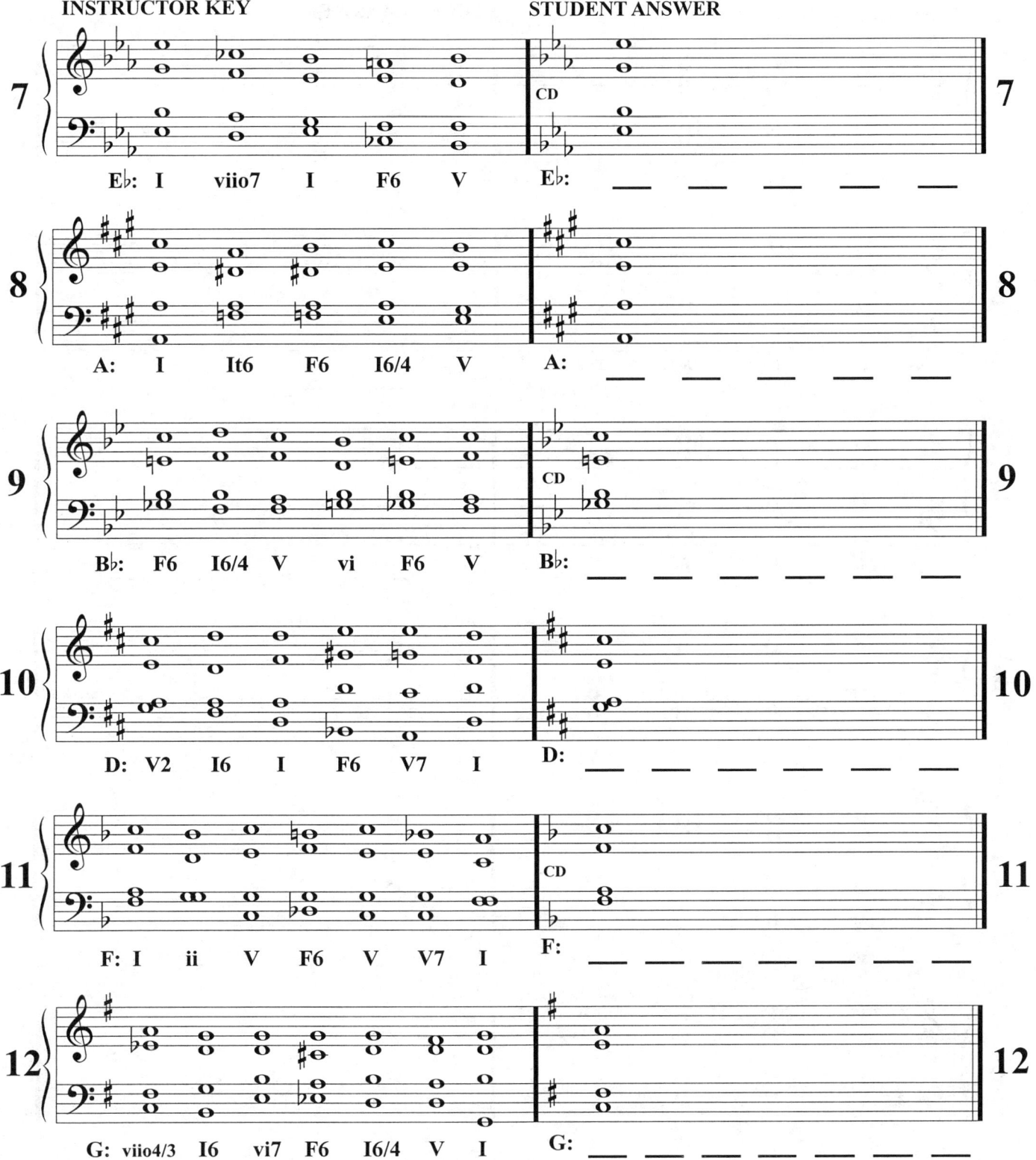

SECTION 9B
Harmony

CD 53

FOCUS: *French sixth*

INSTRUCTOR KEY / STUDENT ANSWER

1. a: i F6 V i
2. a: i F6 i6/4 V7
3. a: i iv F6 V
4. a: i VI7 F6 V
5. a: i6 i F6 i6/4
6. a: i VI F6 V

SECTION 10
Instructor Key

SECTION 10
Student Answer

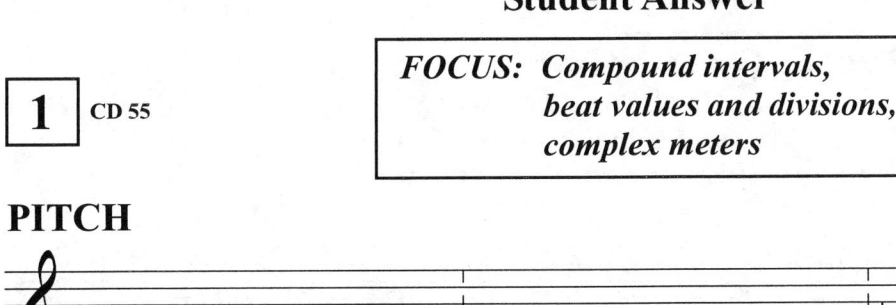

1 CD 55

PITCH

RHYTHM

MELODY

SECTION 10
Instructor Key

2

FOCUS: Compound intervals, beat values and divisions, complex meters

PITCH

RHYTHM

MELODY

SECTION 10
Student Answer

FOCUS: Compound intervals, beat values and divisions, complex meters

2

PITCH

RHYTHM

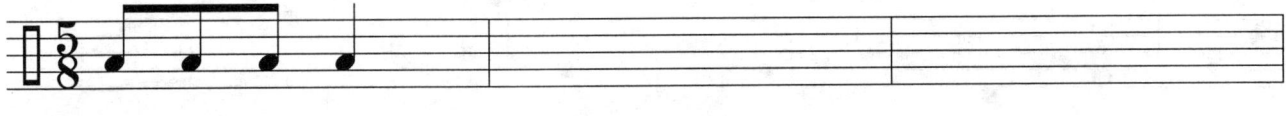

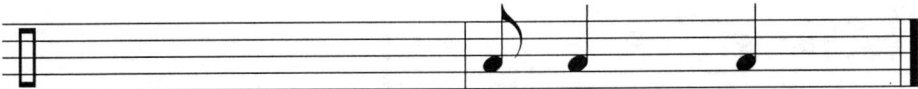

MELODY

SECTION 10
Instructor Key

FOCUS: Compound intervals, beat values and divisions, complex meters

SECTION 10
Student Answer

> *FOCUS: Compound intervals, beat values and divisions, complex meters*

3 CD 56

PITCH

RHYTHM

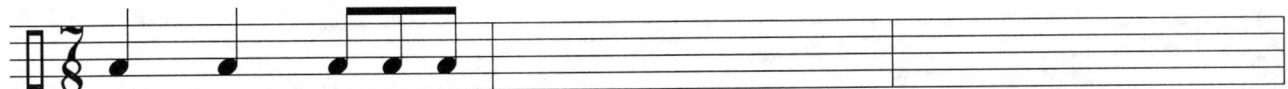

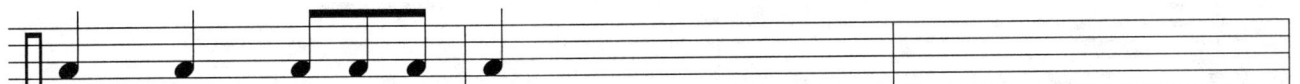

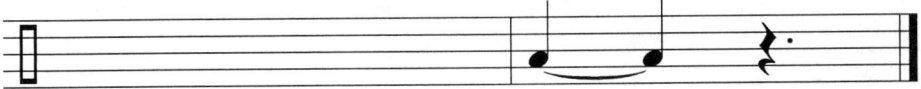

MELODY

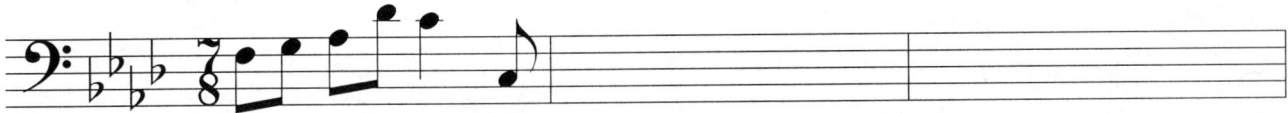

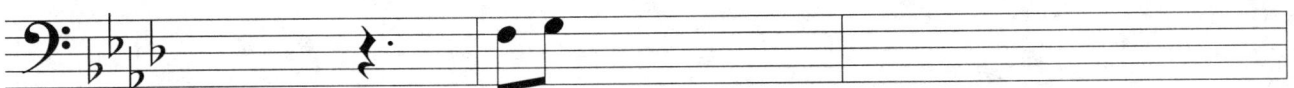

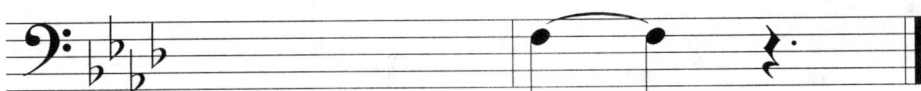

SECTION 10
Instructor Key

FOCUS: Compound intervals, beat values and divisions, complex meters

SECTION 10
Student Answer

FOCUS: Compound intervals, beat values and divisions, complex meters

4

PITCH

RHYTHM

MELODY

CD 57

SECTION 10A
Harmony

FOCUS: *German sixth*

INSTRUCTOR KEY — STUDENT ANSWER

1. C: I — G6 — V — I6   C: ___ ___ ___ ___
2. C: I — G6 — I6/4 — V   C: ___ ___ ___ ___
3. C: I — I7 — G6 — V   C: ___ ___ ___ ___
4. C: V7 — I — G6 — V   C: ___ ___ ___ ___
5. C: I — V — G6 — V   C: ___ ___ ___ ___
6. C: G6 — G6 — I6/4 — V7   C: ___ ___ ___ ___

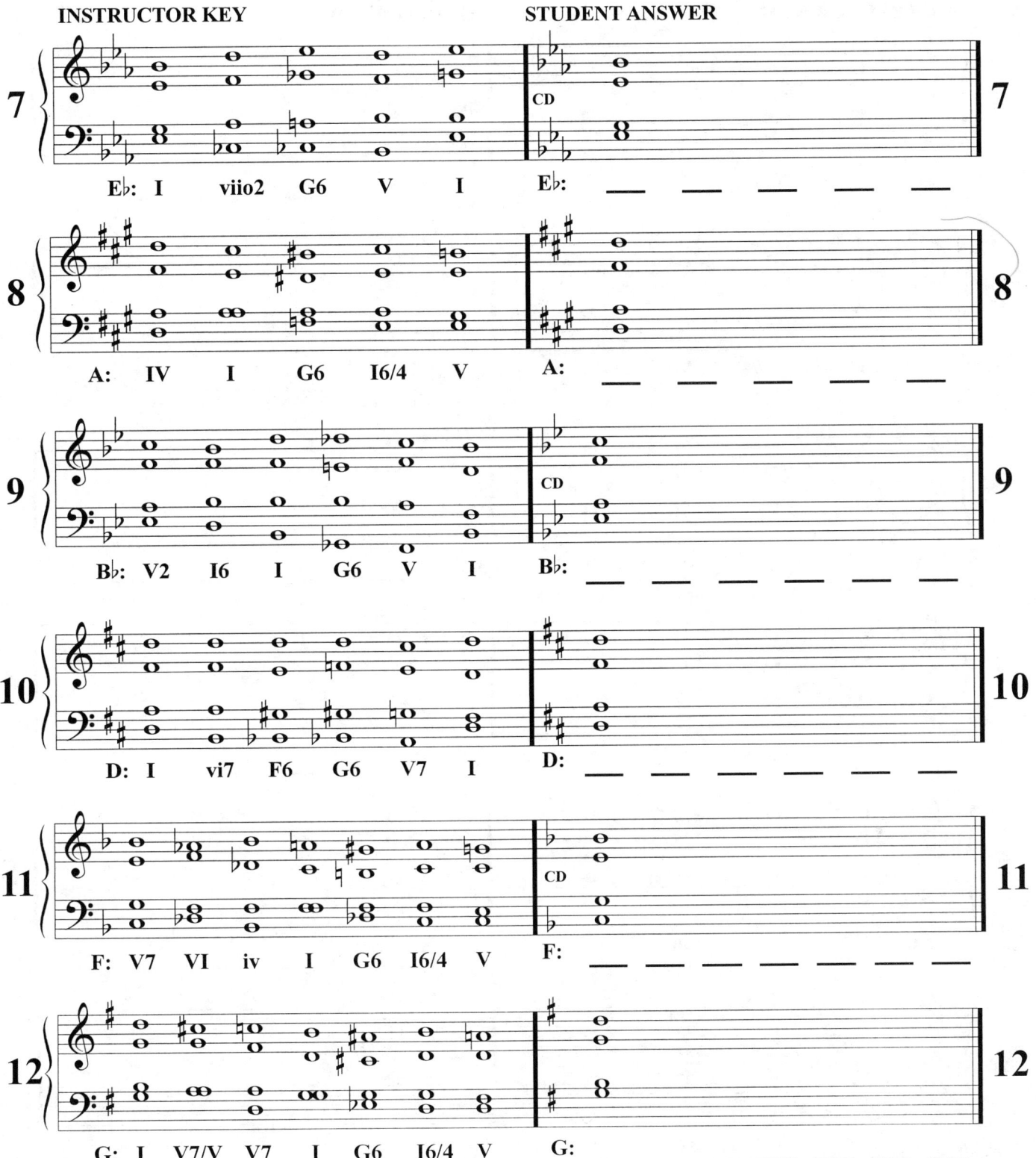

SECTION 10B
Harmony

FOCUS: *German sixth*

INSTRUCTOR KEY — **STUDENT ANSWER**

1. a: i G6 V i — a: ___ ___ ___ ___
2. a: i G6 V7 i — a: ___ ___ ___ ___
3. a: i G6 i6/4 V — a: ___ ___ ___ ___
4. a: i iv6/5 G6 V — a: ___ ___ ___ ___
5. a: V i G6 i6/4 — a: ___ ___ ___ ___
6. a: i VI7 G6 V — a: ___ ___ ___ ___

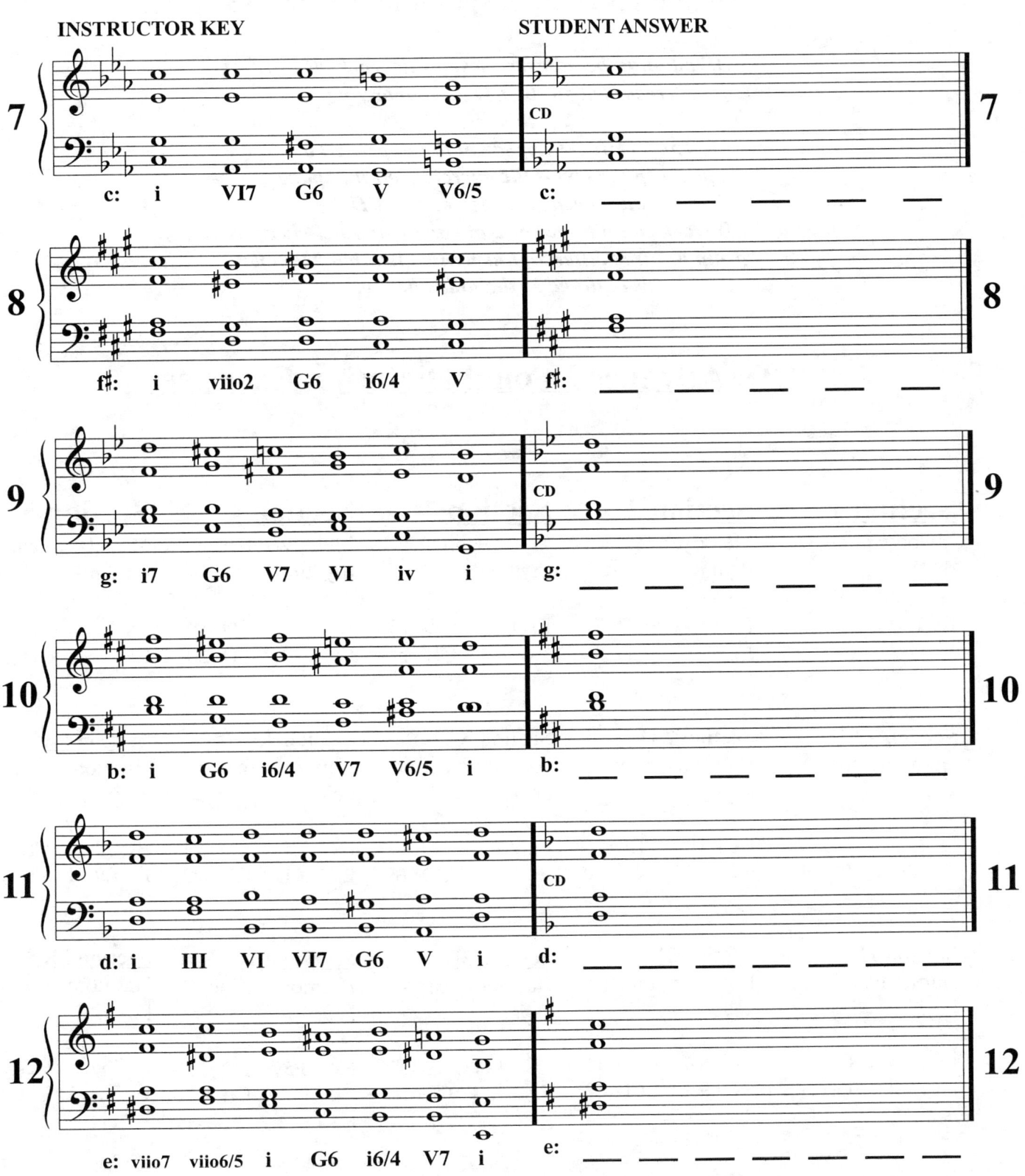

CD Index
to exercises & corresponding CD tracks

*All odd-numbered exercises in this workbook are
recorded on the CD accompanying
this text.
The CD tracks appear in the upper left of
pages in the text if the exercises on that page
have been recorded on the CD.
Each CD track contains either a pitch/rhythm/melody exercise
group or three different harmonic dictation examples
as outlined in the index below.*

CD: Advanced Tonal Dictation Exercises

Section 1	Section 2	Section 3	Section 4	Section 5
Melody, pitch, rhythm	Melody, pitch, rhythm	Melody, pitch, rhythm	Melody, pitch, rhythm	Melody, pitch, rhythm
Ex 1 CD 1	Ex 1 CD 7	Ex 1 CD 13	Ex 1 CD 19	Ex 1 CD 25
Ex 3 CD 2	Ex 3 CD 8	Ex 3 CD 14	Ex 3 CD 20	Ex 3 CD 26
Section 1A	**Section 2A**	**Section 3A**	**Section 4A**	**Section 5A**
Harmony, major keys	Harmony, major keys	Harmony, major keys	Harmony, major keys	Harmony, major keys
Ex 1,3,5 CD 3	Ex 1,3,5 CD 9	Ex 1,3,5 CD 15	Ex 1,3,5 CD 21	Ex 1,3,5 CD 27
Ex 7,9,11 CD 4	Ex 7,9,11 CD 10	Ex 7,9,11 CD 16	Ex 7,9,11 CD 22	Ex 7,9,11 CD 28
Section 1B	**Section 2B**	**Section 3B**	**Section 4B**	**Section 5B**
Harmony, minor keys	Harmony, minor keys	Harmony, minor keys	Harmony, minor keys	Harmony, minor keys
Ex 1,3,5 CD 5	Ex 1,3,5 CD 11	Ex 1,3,5 CD 17	Ex 1,3,5 CD 23	Ex 13,5 CD 29
Ex 7,9,11 CD 6	Ex 7,9,11 CD 12	Ex 7,9,11 CD 18	Ex 7,9,11 CD 24	Ex 7,9,11 CD 30

CD: Advanced Tonal Dictation Exercises, continued

Section 6 Melody, pitch, rhythm	**Section 7** Melody, pitch, rhythm	**Section 8** Melody, pitch, rhythm	**Section 9** Melody, pitch, rhythm	**Section 10** Melody, pitch, rhythm
Ex 1 CD 31	Ex 1 CD 37	Ex 1 CD 43	Ex 1 CD 49	Ex 1 CD 55
Ex 3 CD 32	Ex 3 CD 38	Ex 3 CD 44	Ex 3 CD 50	Ex 3 CD 56
Section 6A Harmony, major keys	**Section 7A** Harmony, major keys	**Section 8A** Harmony, major keys	**Section 9A** Harmony, major keys	**Section 10A** Harmony, major keys
Ex 1,3,5 CD 33	Ex 1,3,5 CD 39	Ex 1,3,5 CD 45	Ex 1,3,5 CD 51	Ex 1,3,5 CD 57
Ex 7,9,11 CD 34	Ex 7,9,11 CD 40	Ex 7,9,11 CD 46	Ex 7,9,11 CD 52	Ex 7,9,11 CD 58
Section 6B Harmony, minor keys	**Section 7B** Harmony, minor keys	**Section 8B** Harmony, minor keys	**Section 9B** Harmony, minor keys	**Section 10B** Harmony, minor keys
Ex 1,3,5 CD 35	Ex 1,3,5 CD 41	Ex 1,3,5 CD 47	Ex 1,3,5 CD 53	Ex 1,3,5 CD 59
Ex 7,9,11 CD 36	Ex 7,9,11 CD 42	Ex 7,9,11 CD 48	Ex 7,9,11 CD 54	Ex 7,9,11 CD 60

About the Author

THOMAS L. DURHAM has taught ear training at Brigham Young University for more than a quarter century. Dozens of schools and universities throughout the United States and Canada have used his dictation materials. Dr. Durham received his B.M. and M.M. degrees from the University of Utah in 1974 and 1975 respectively, and his Ph.D. from the University of Iowa in 1978.

He has consulted with the Advanced Placement's Music Theory division of the College Board since 1996. His catalog of published compositions includes several choral arrangements that are in current use and have been broadcast and performed throughout the world. For each of the past thirteen years, the Standard Awards Panel of the American Society of Composers, Authors, and Publishers (ASCAP) has cited him. From 1980-2002, he sang baritone with the Mormon Tabernacle Choir. During the past two decades, this world-famous chorus premiered many of his choral compositions and arrangements over CBS radio on the choir's weekly "Music and the Spoken Word" program.

Dr. Durham currently serves as Associate Director of the School of Music at Brigham Young University, and as Executive Director of the Barlow Endowment for Music Composition. He lives with his wife Becky in Sandy, Utah.